DRESSES COLORING BOOK

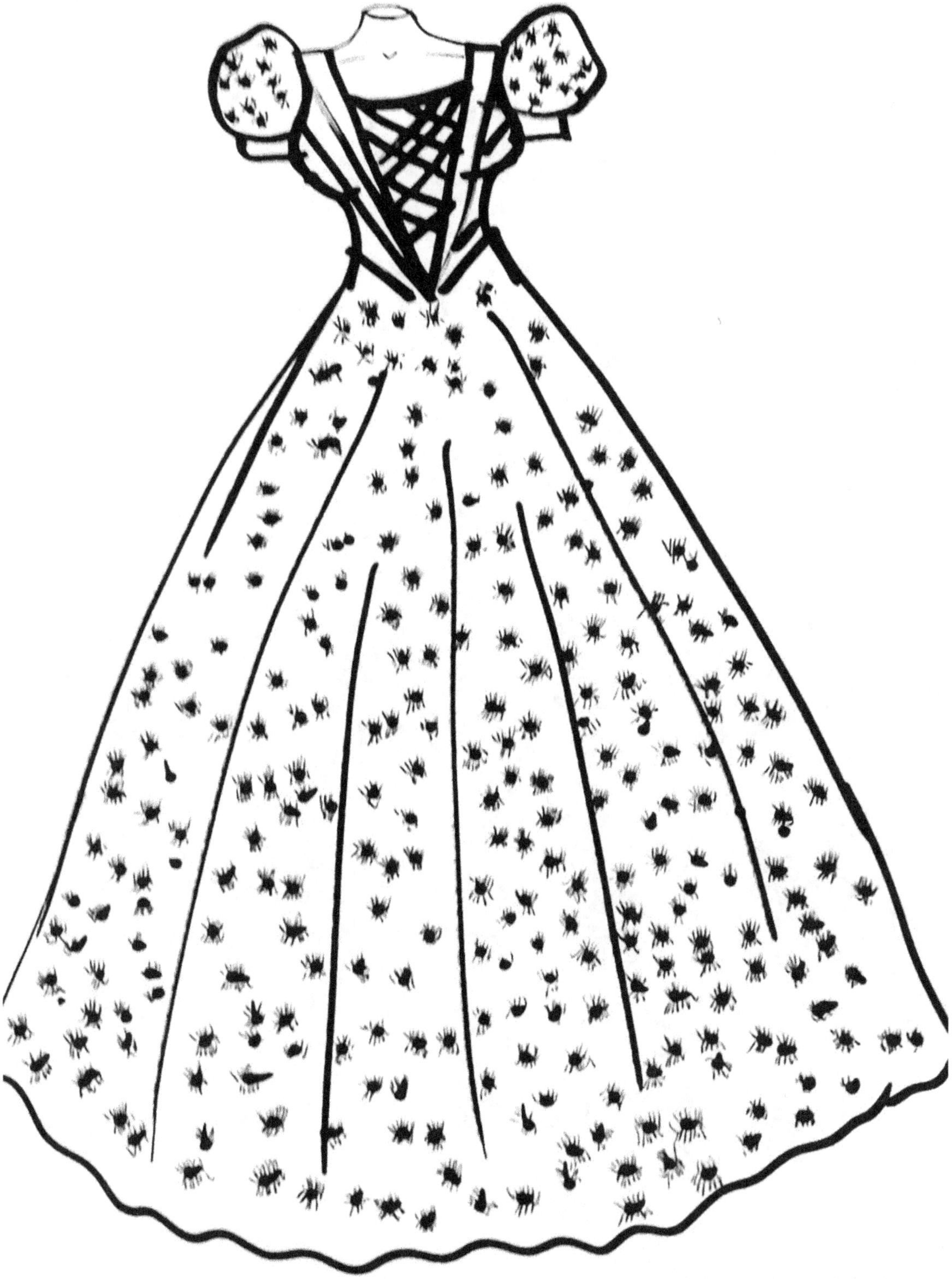

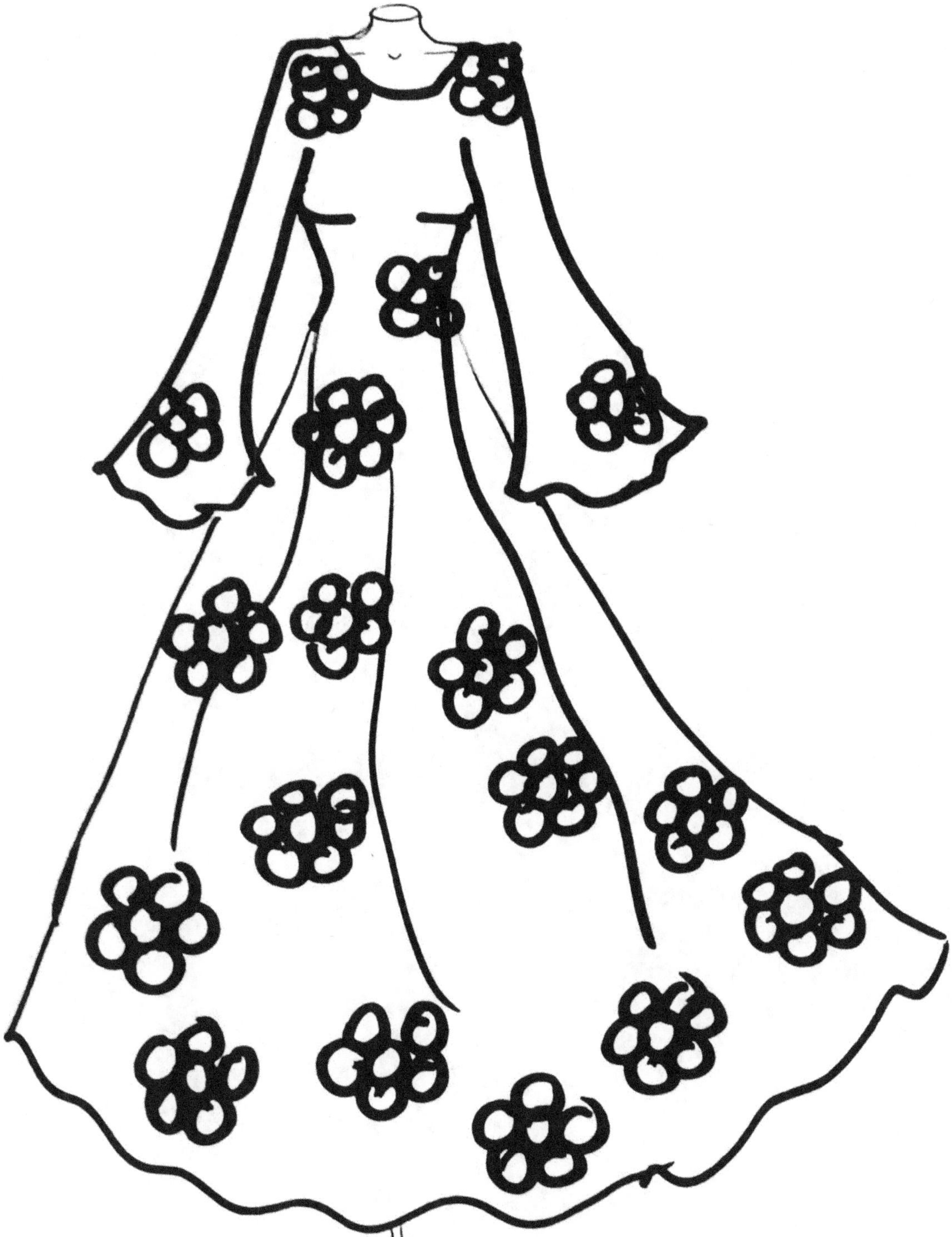

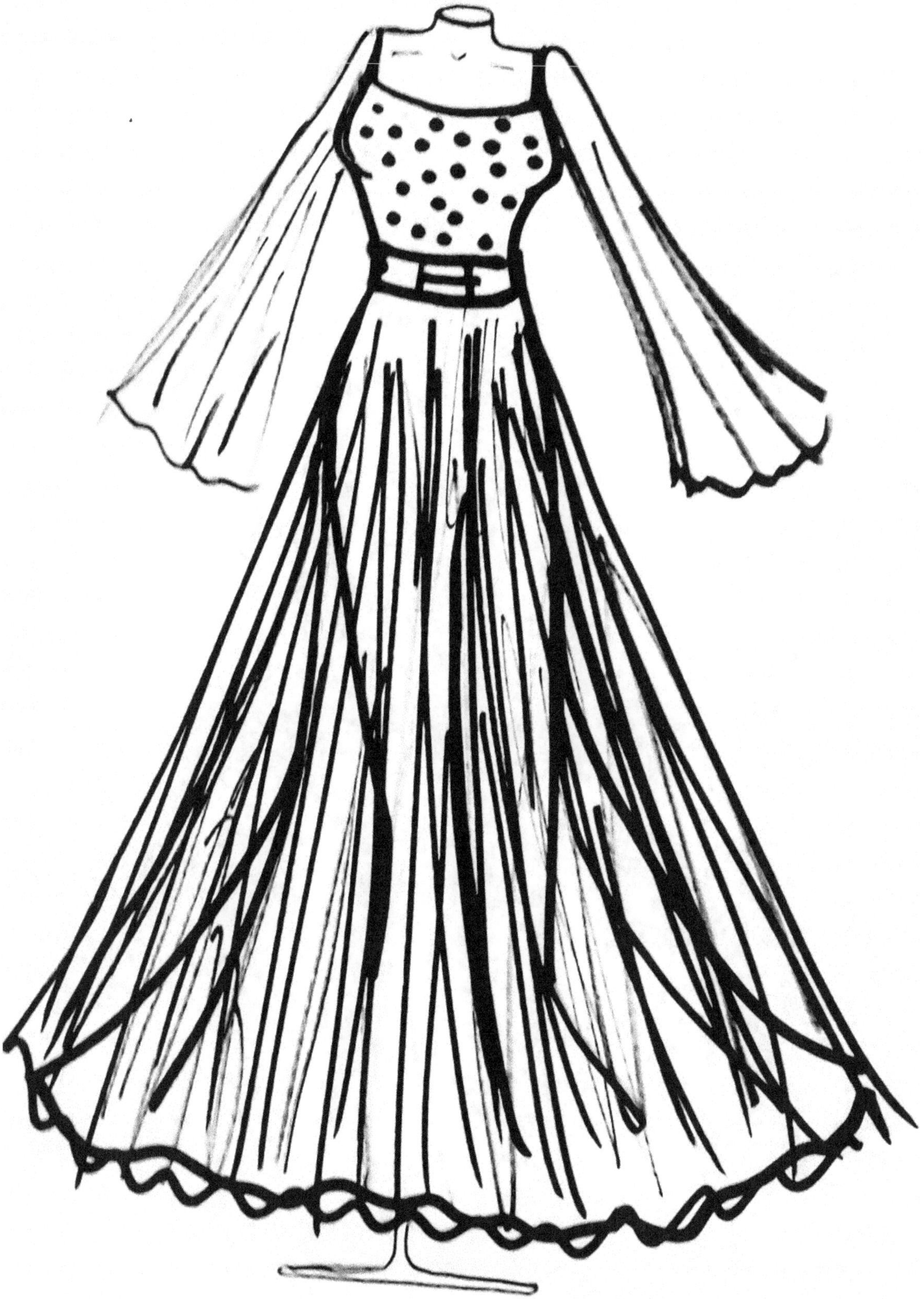

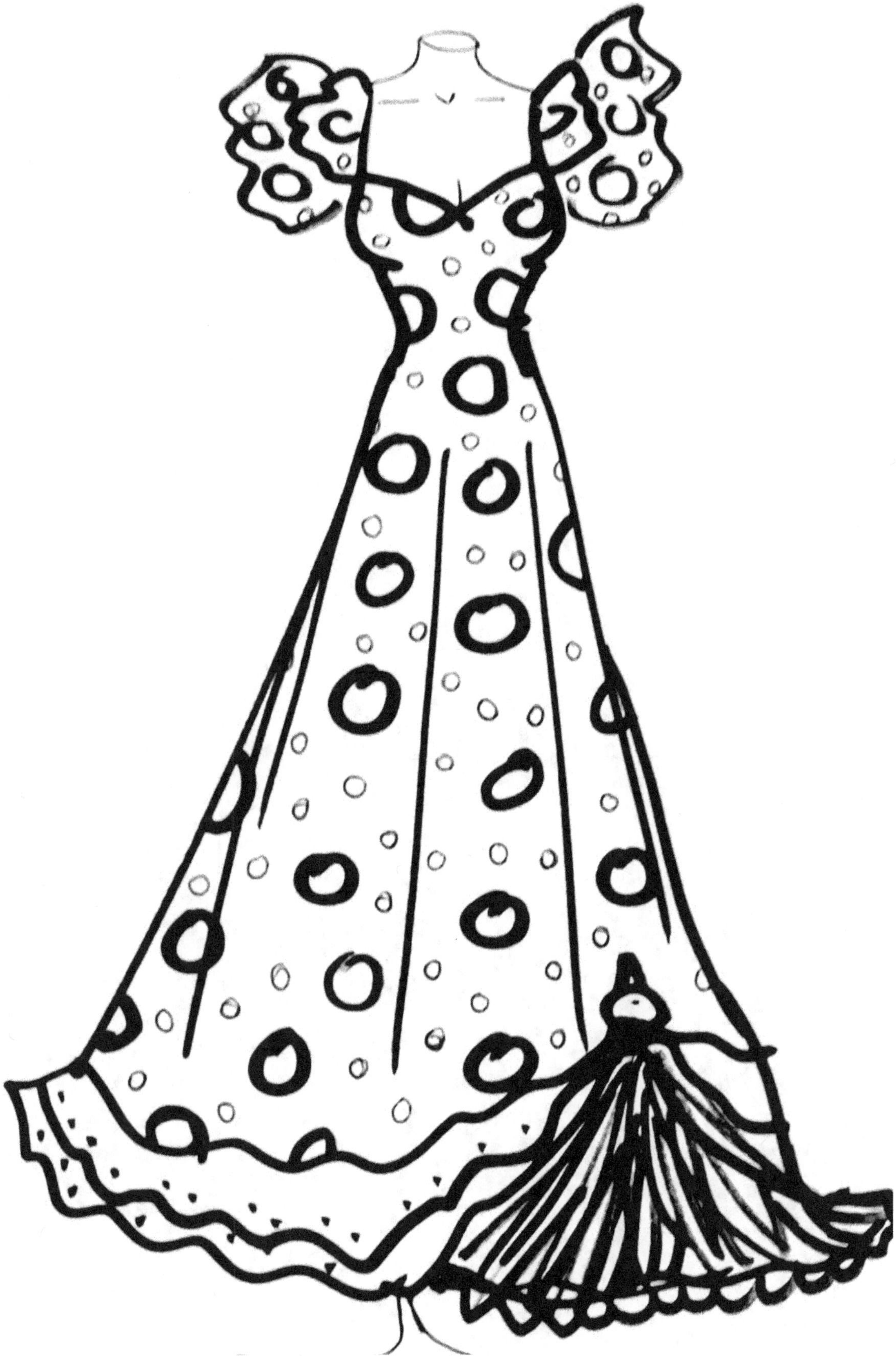

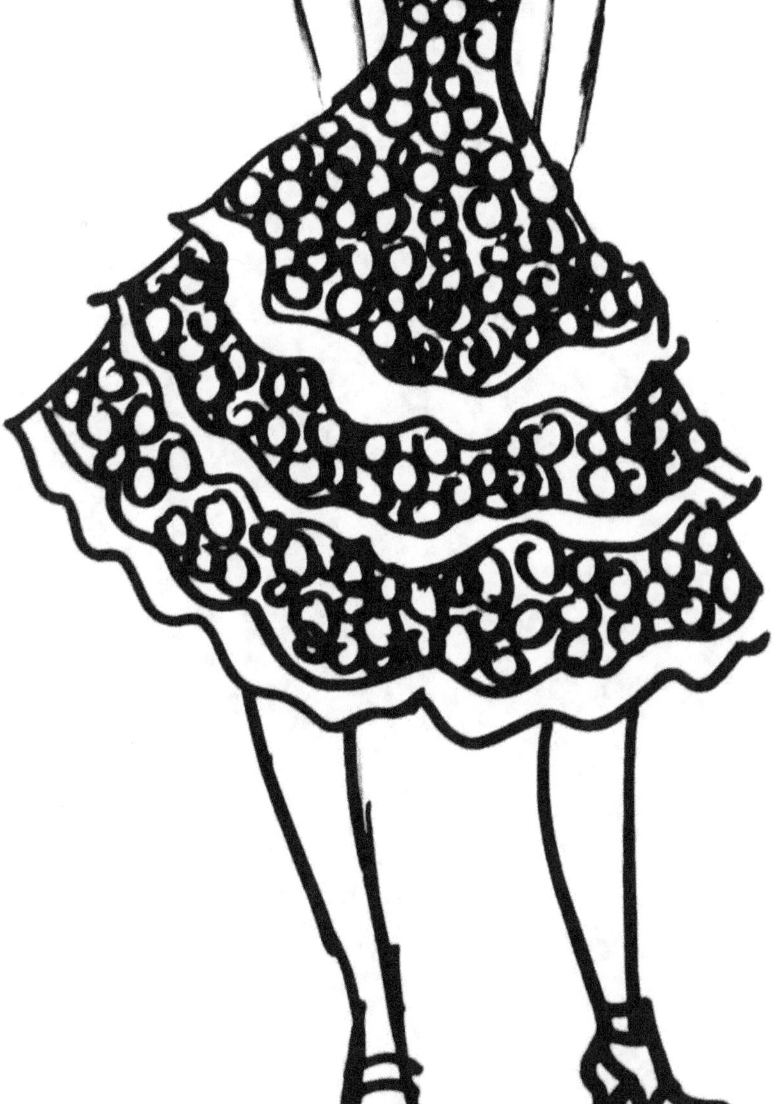

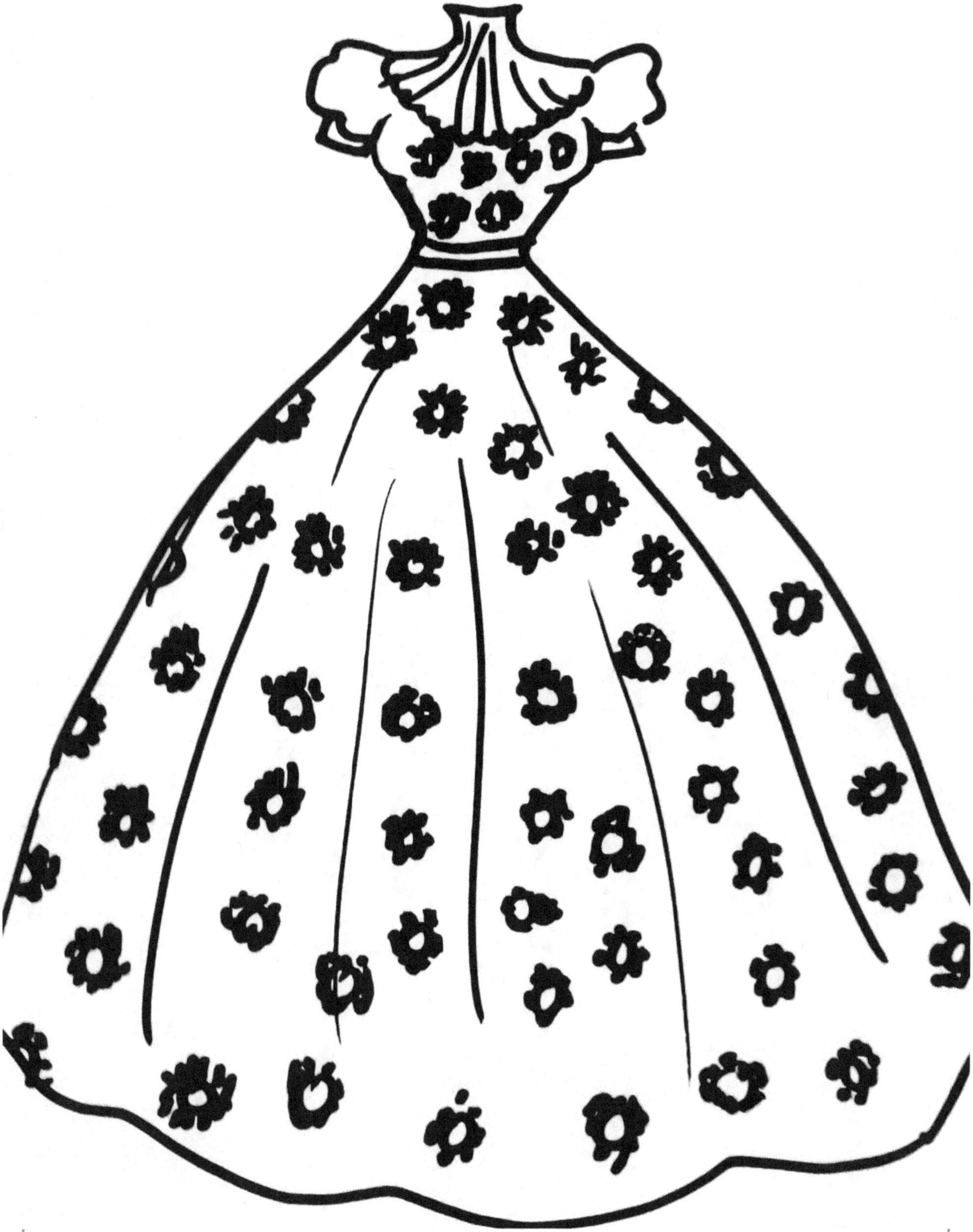

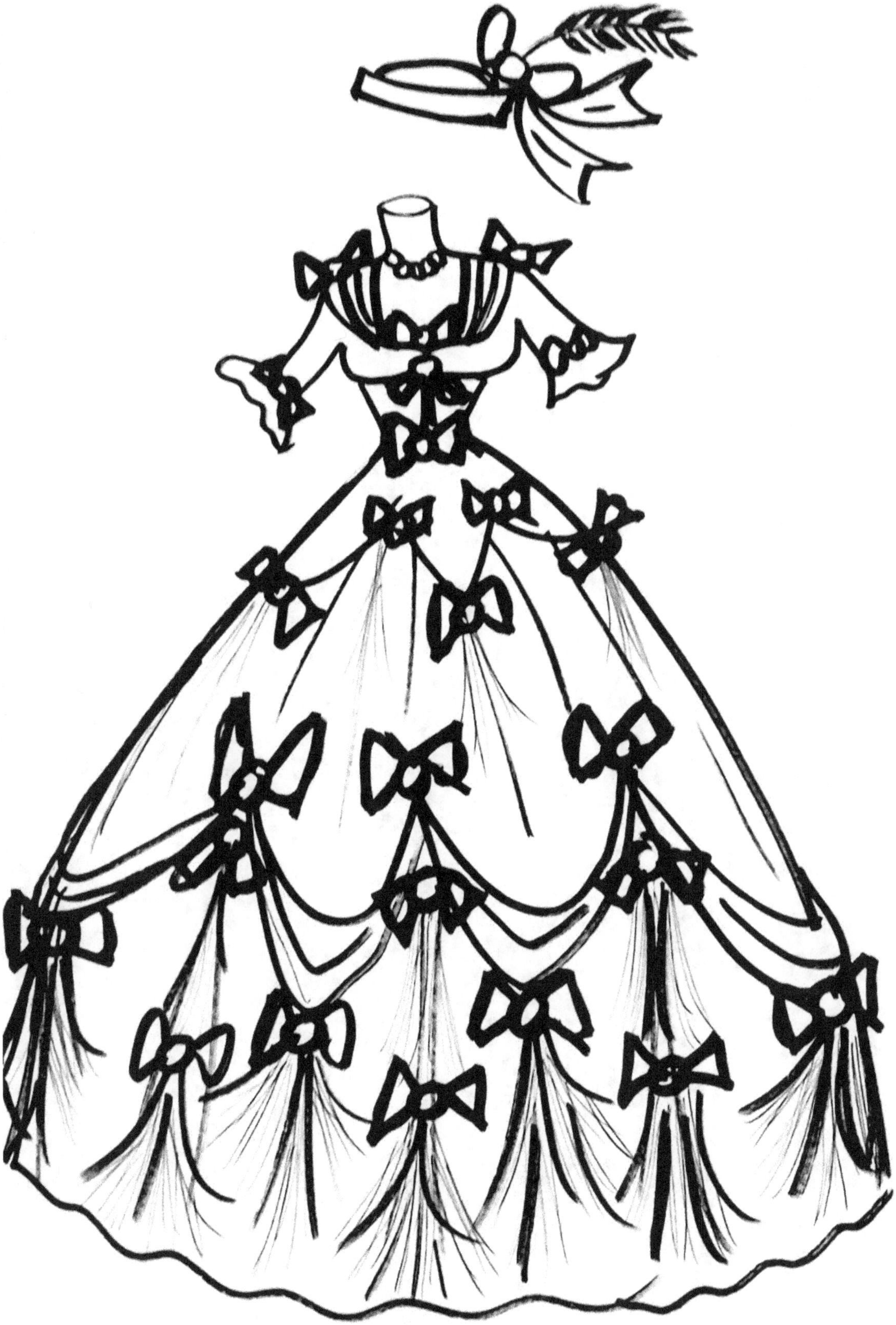

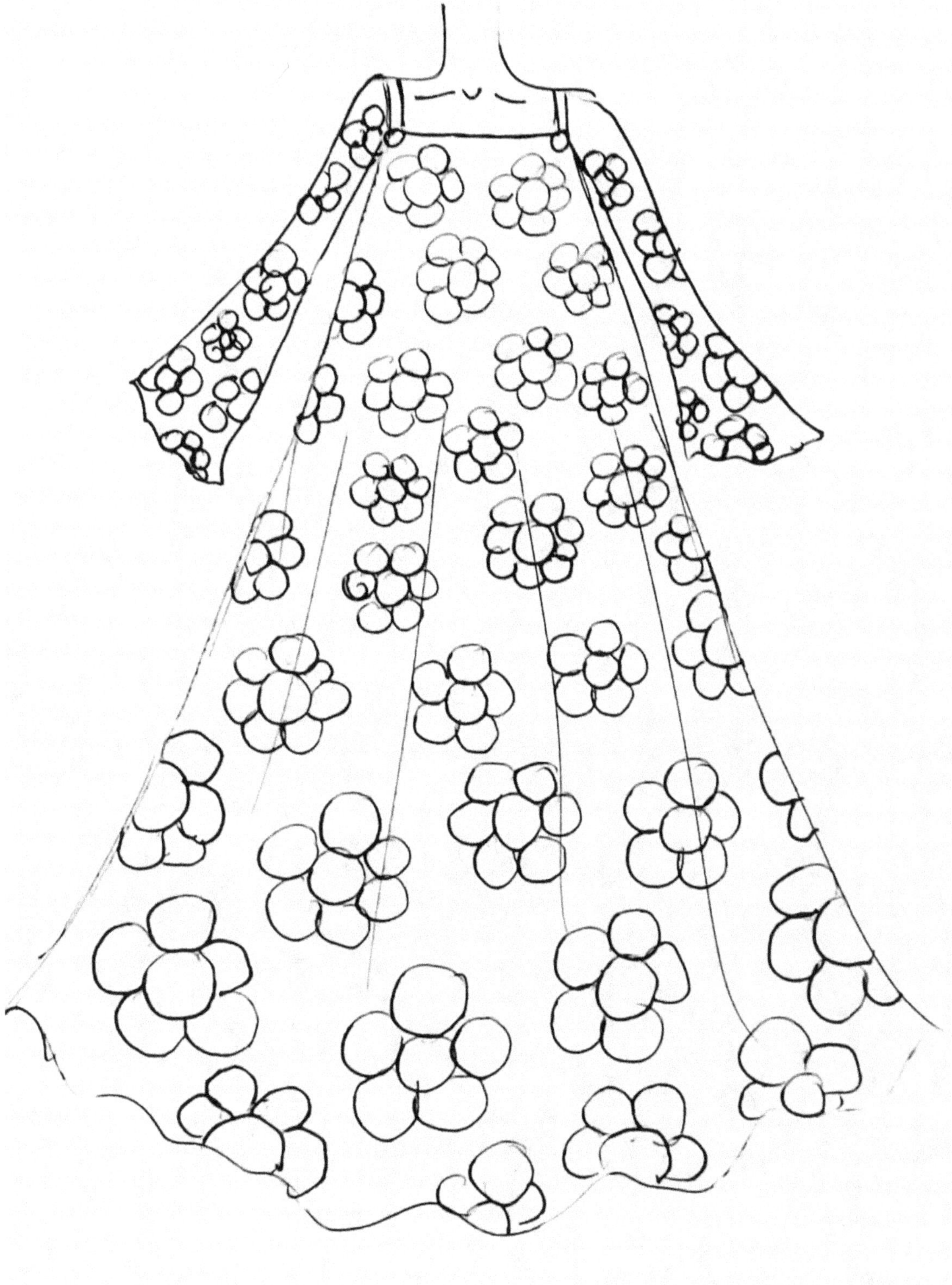

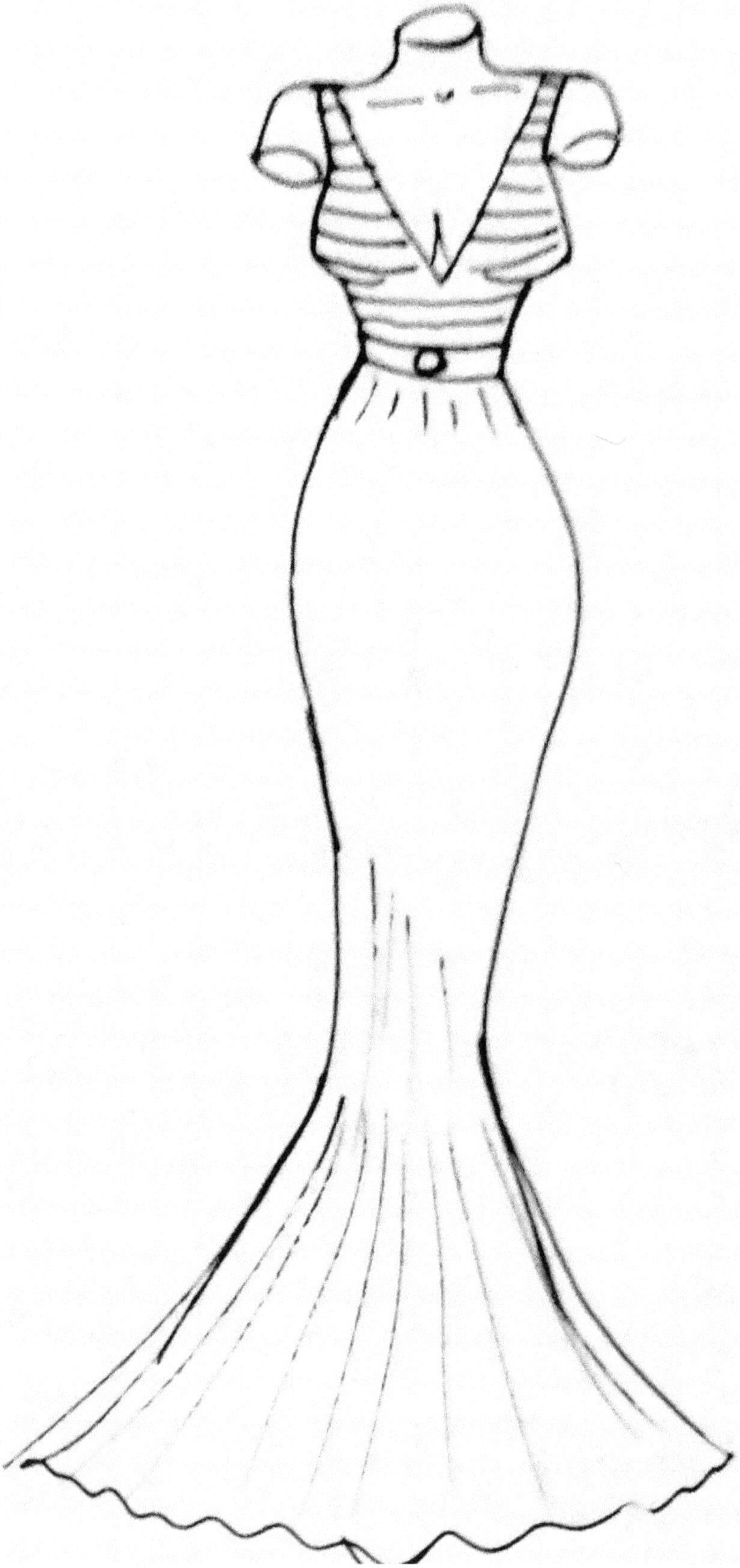

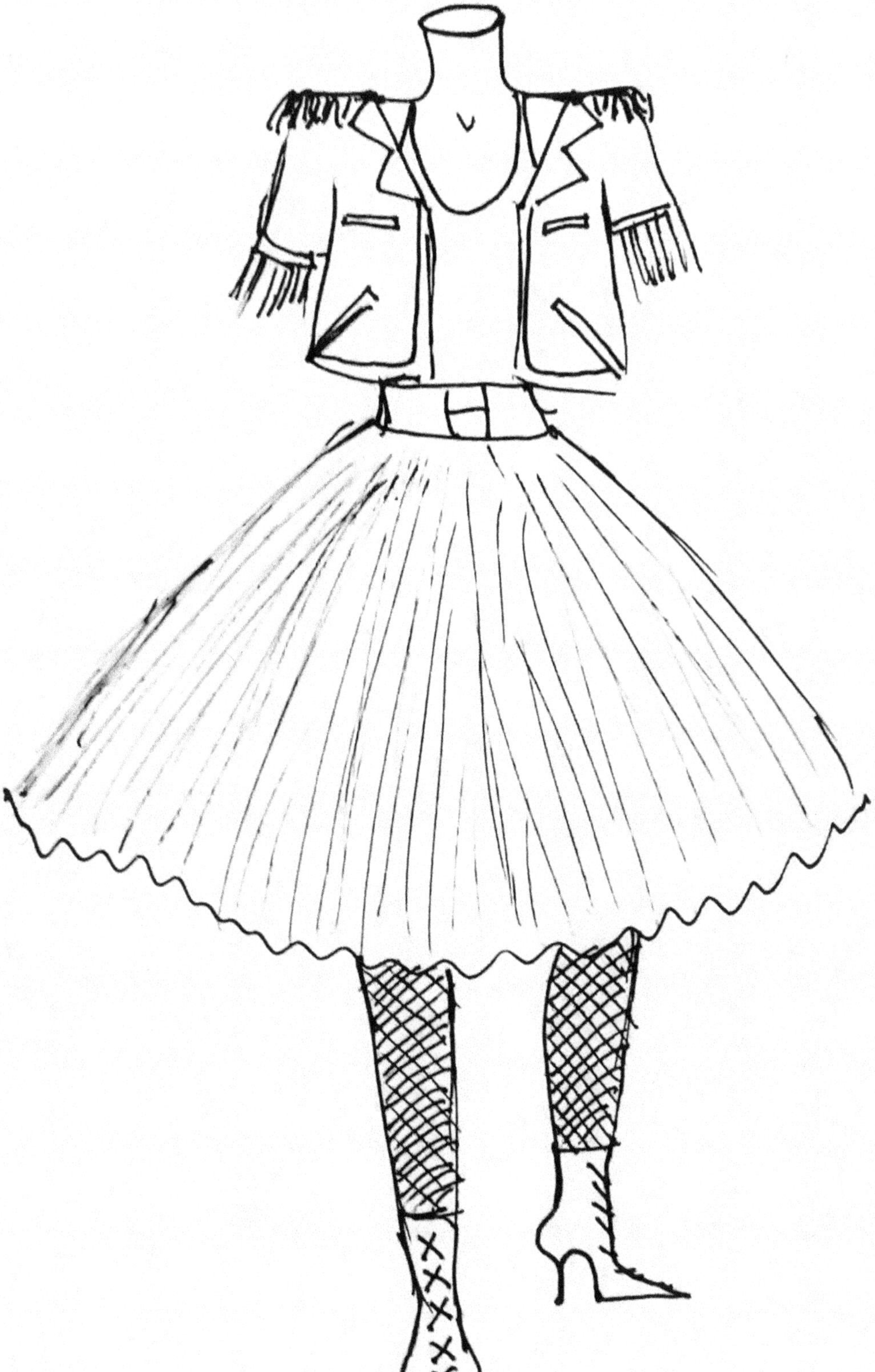

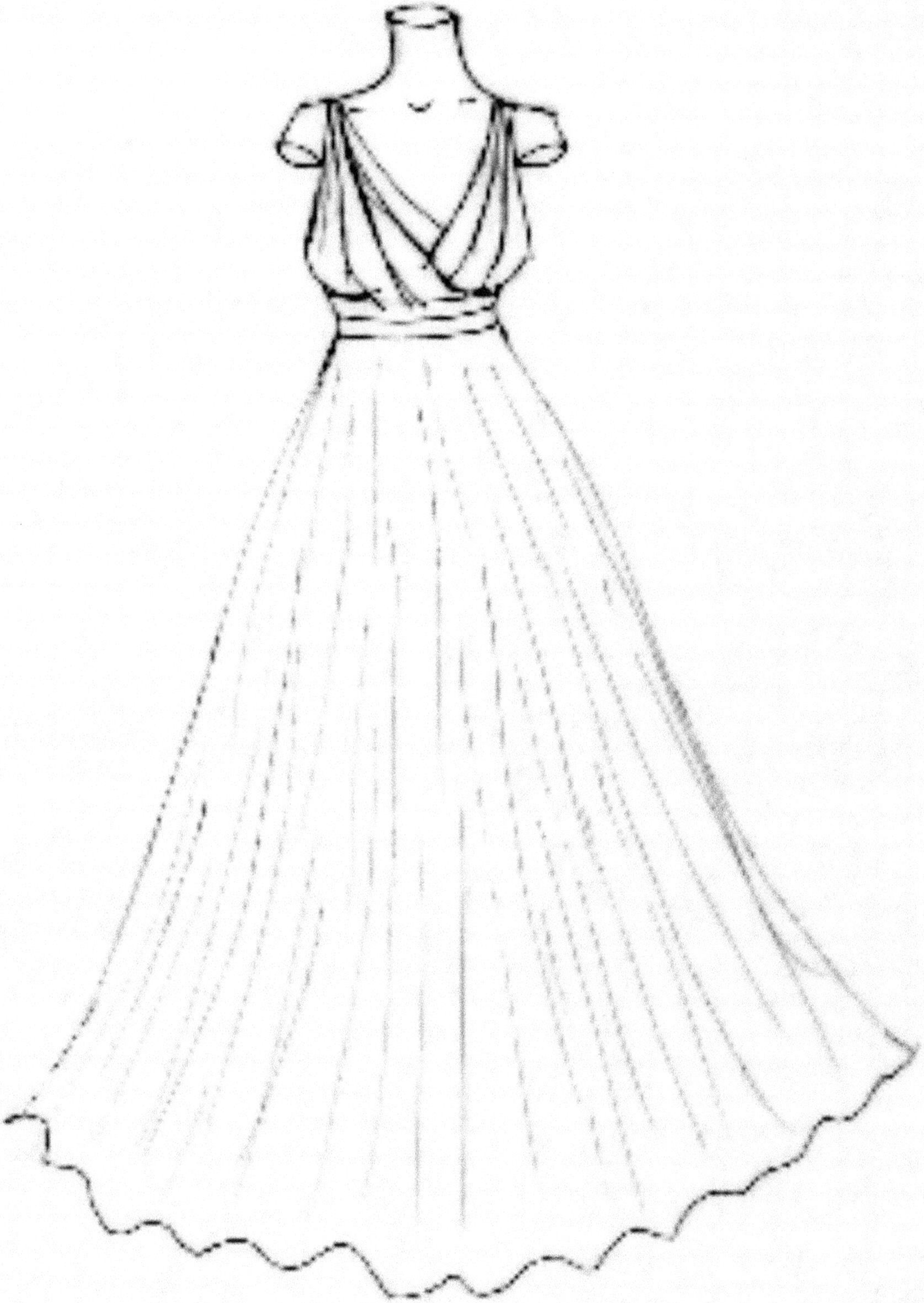

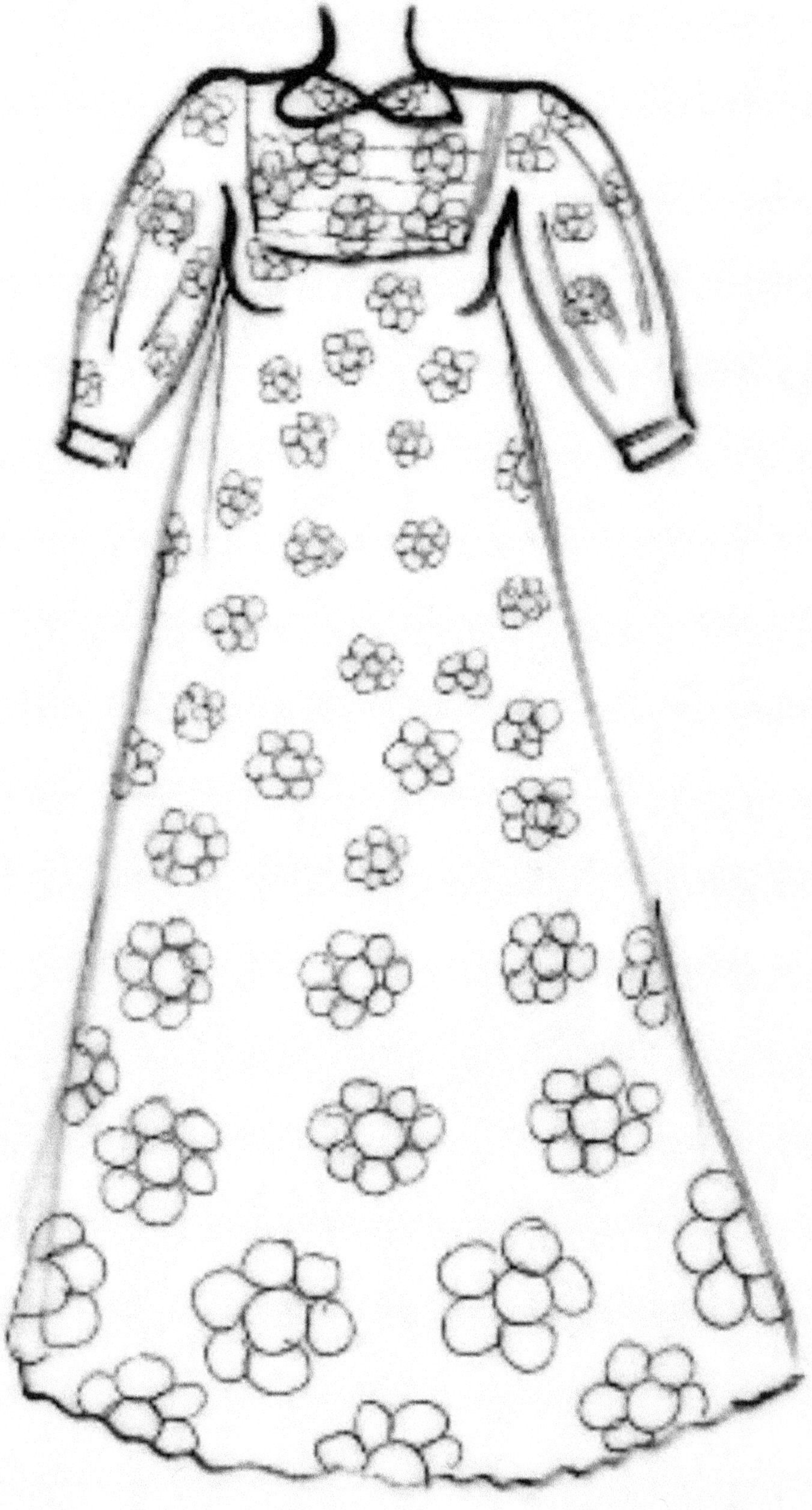

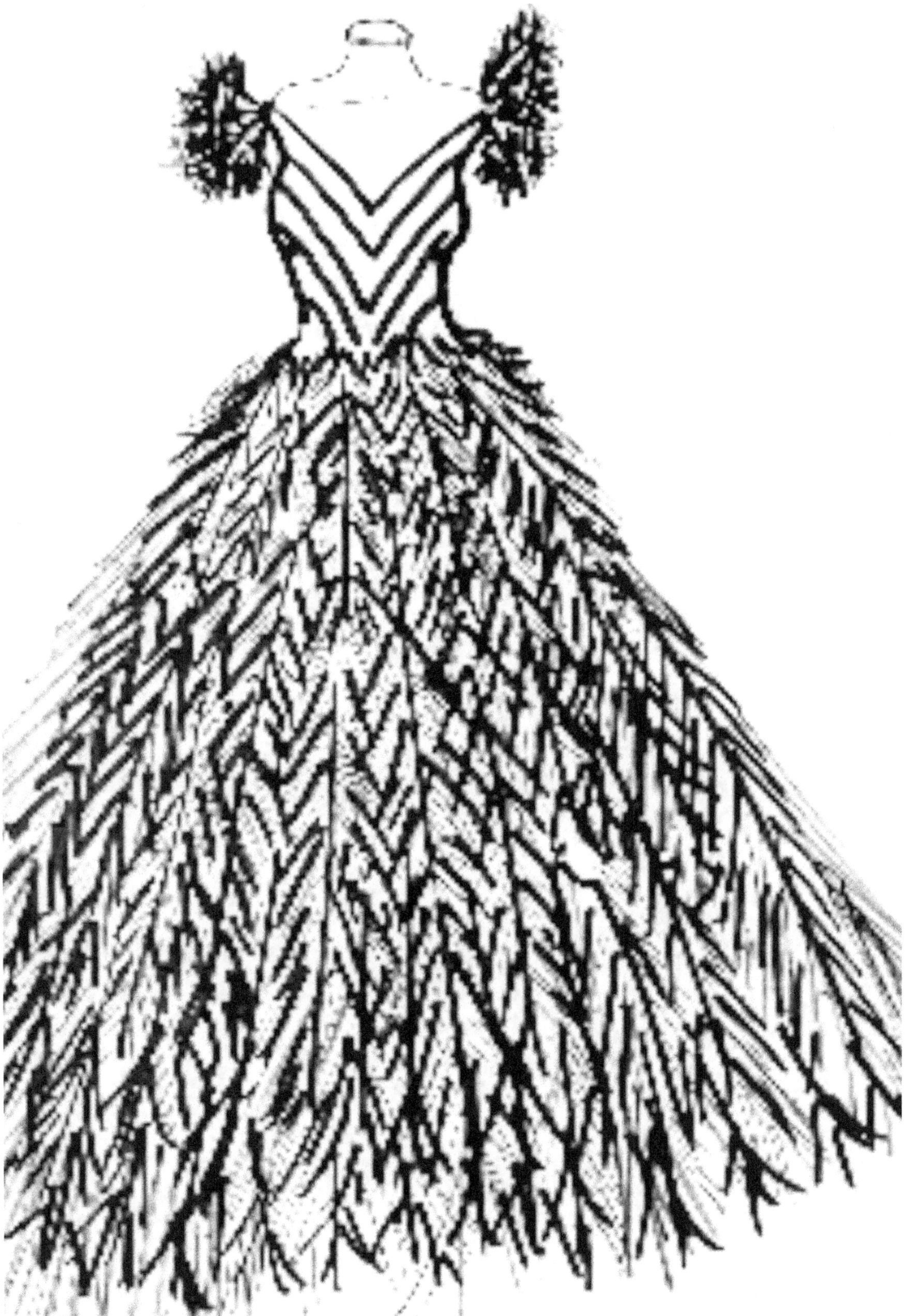

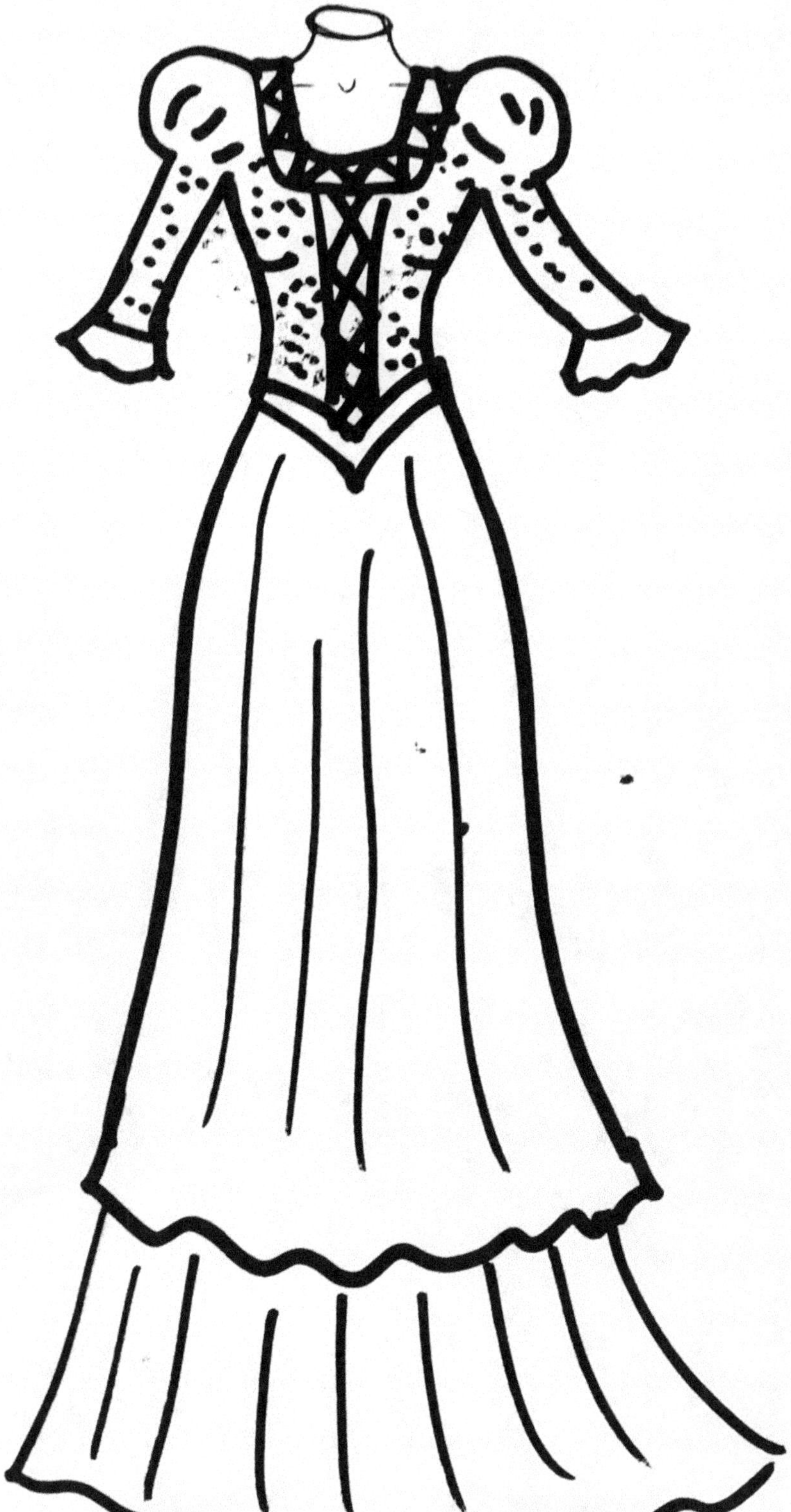

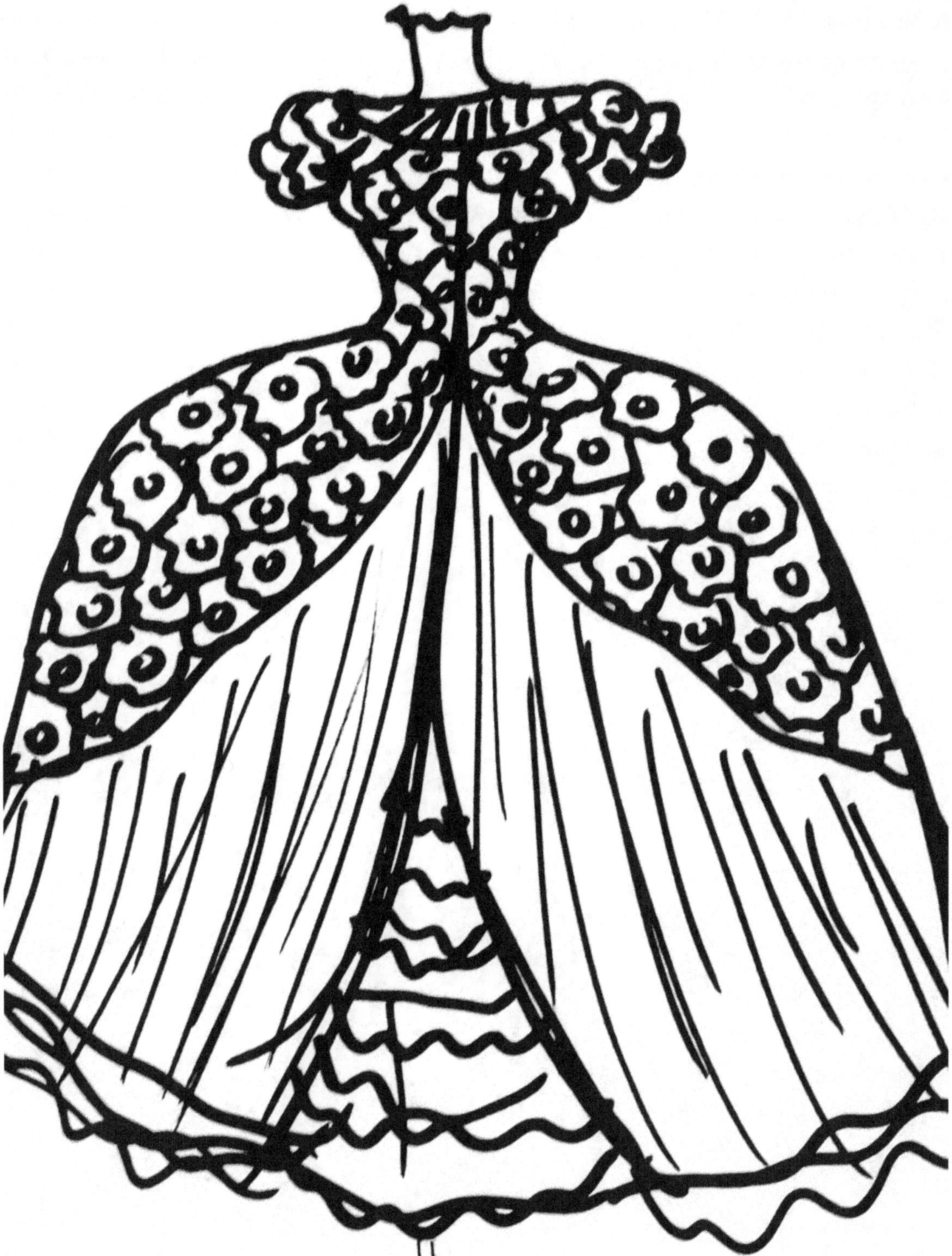

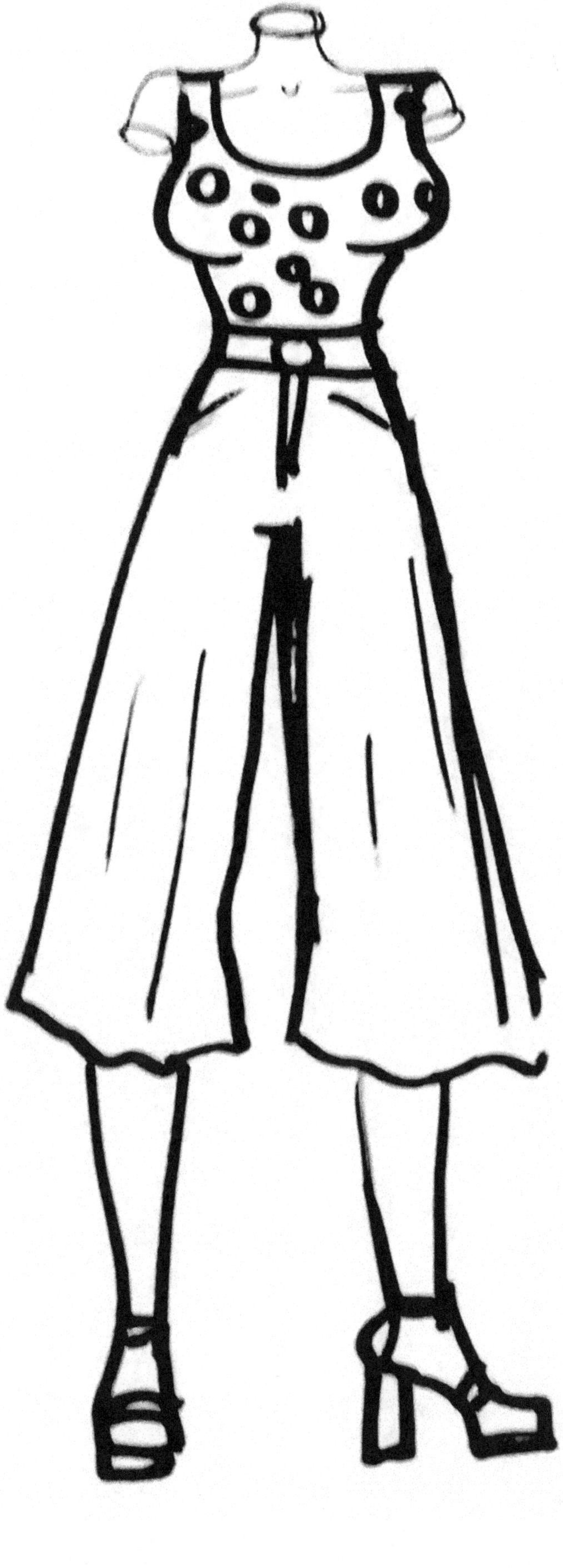

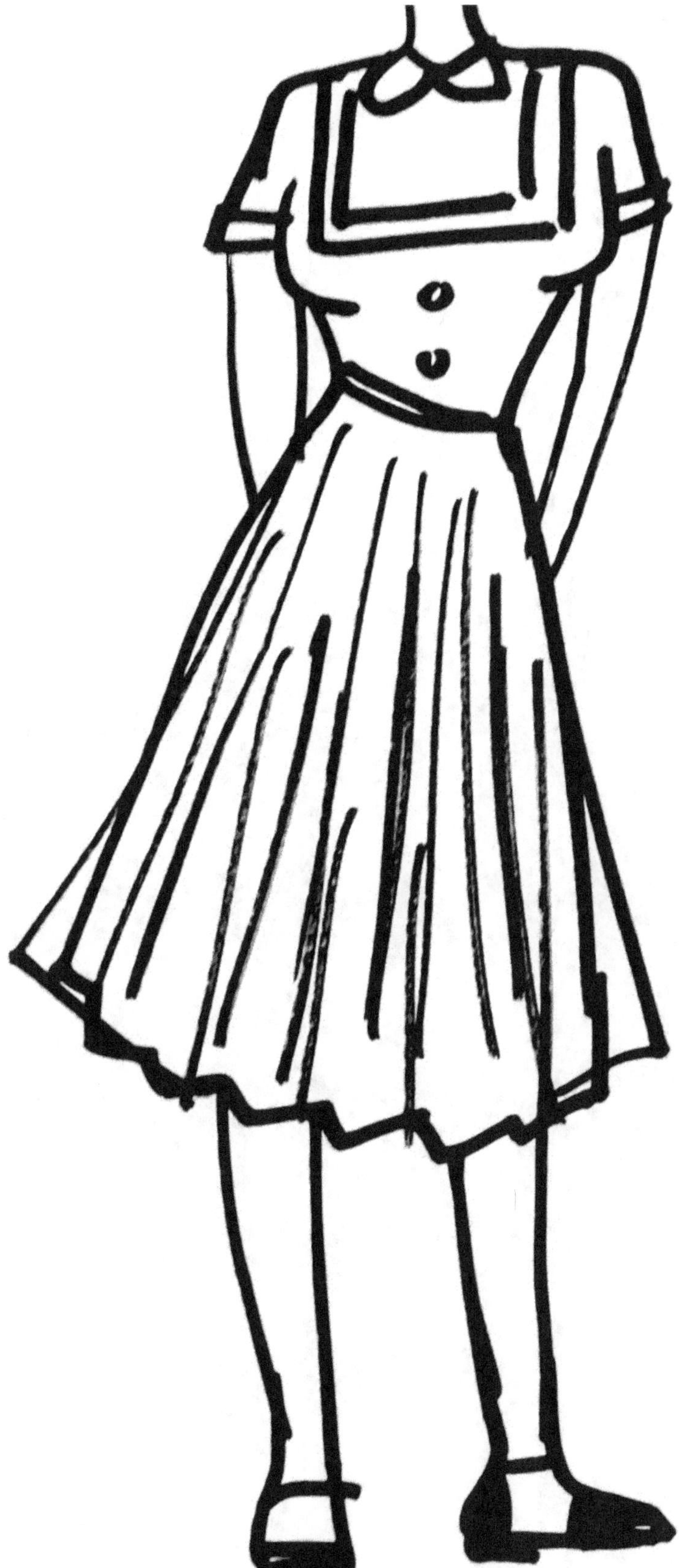

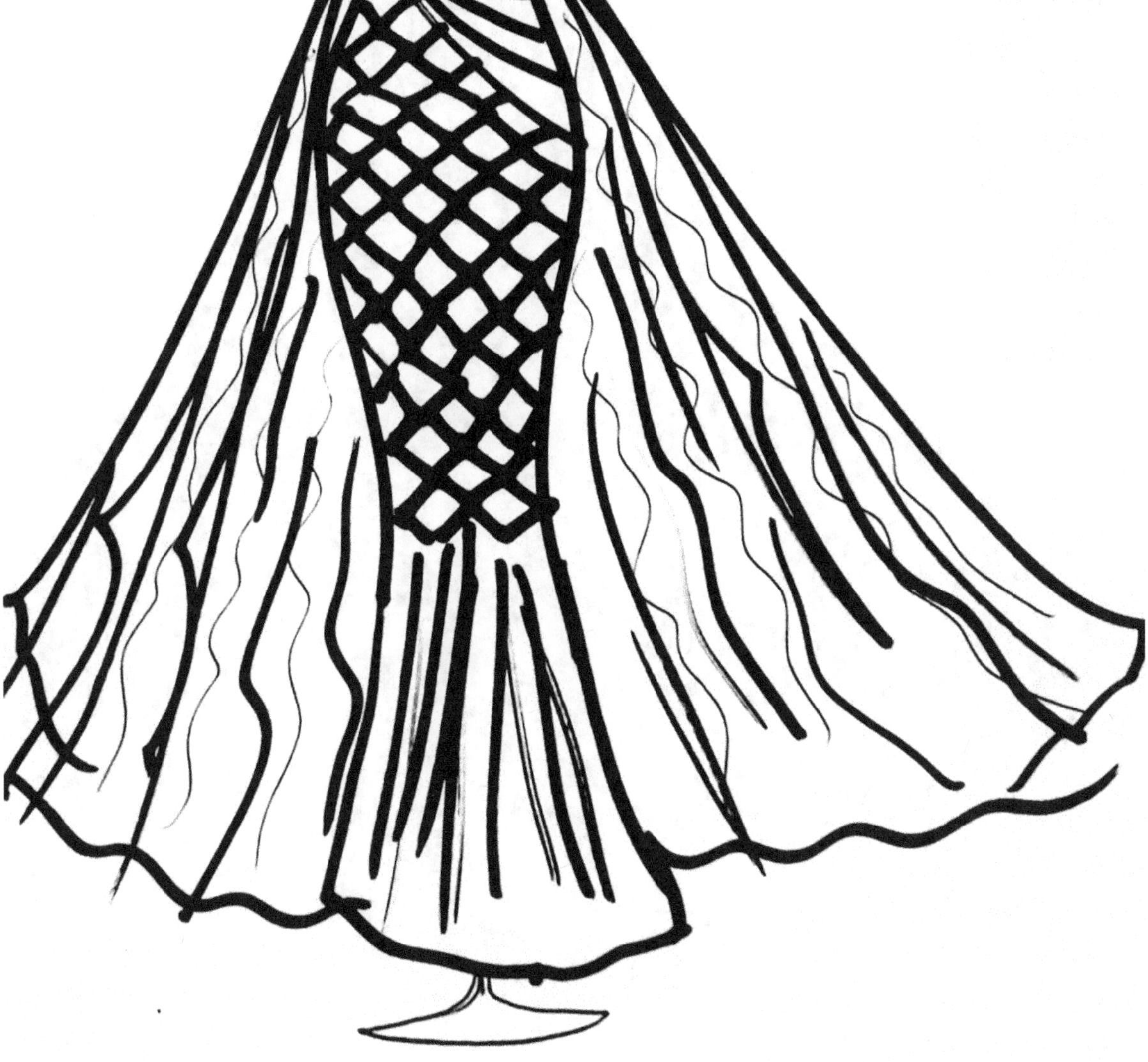

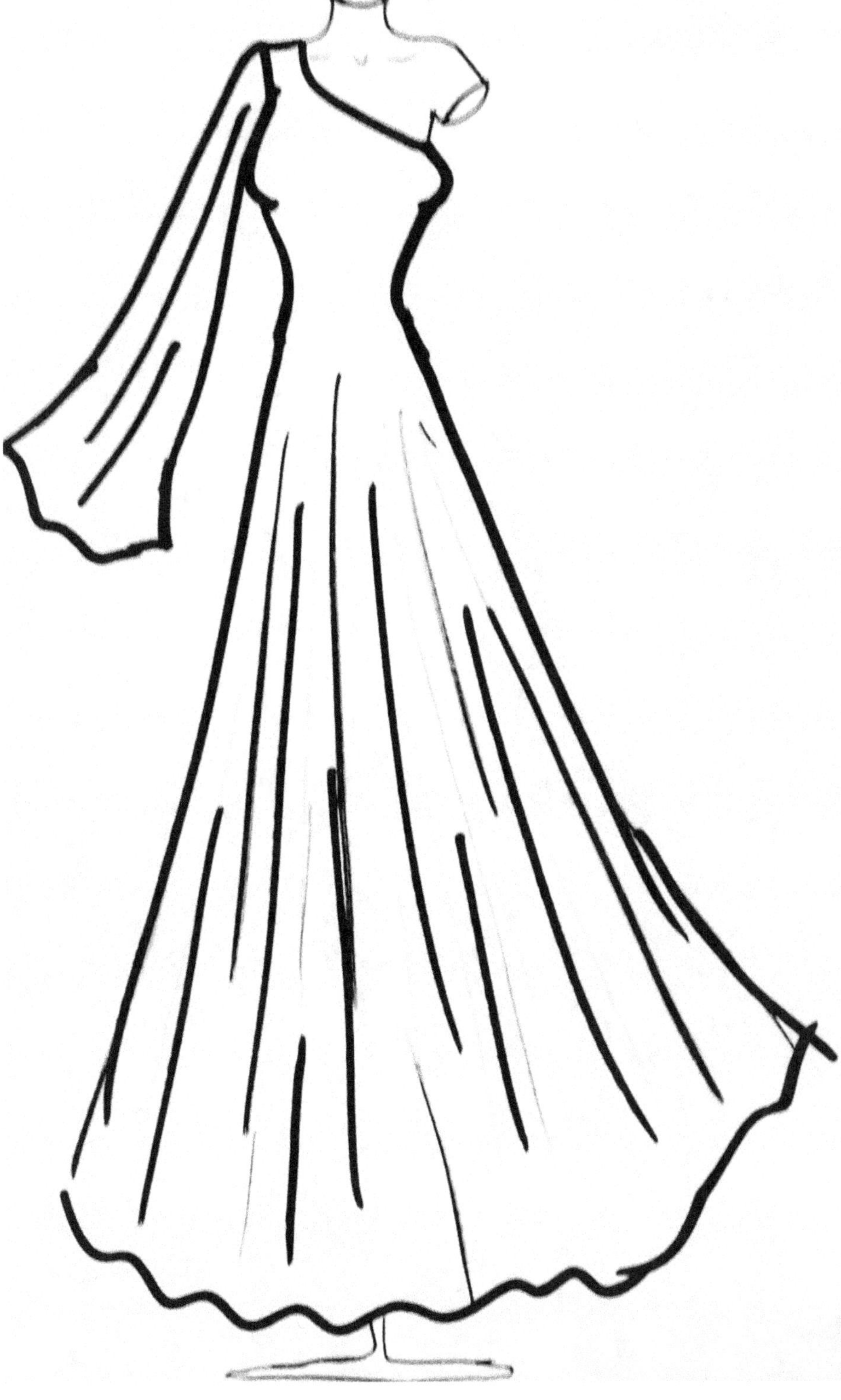

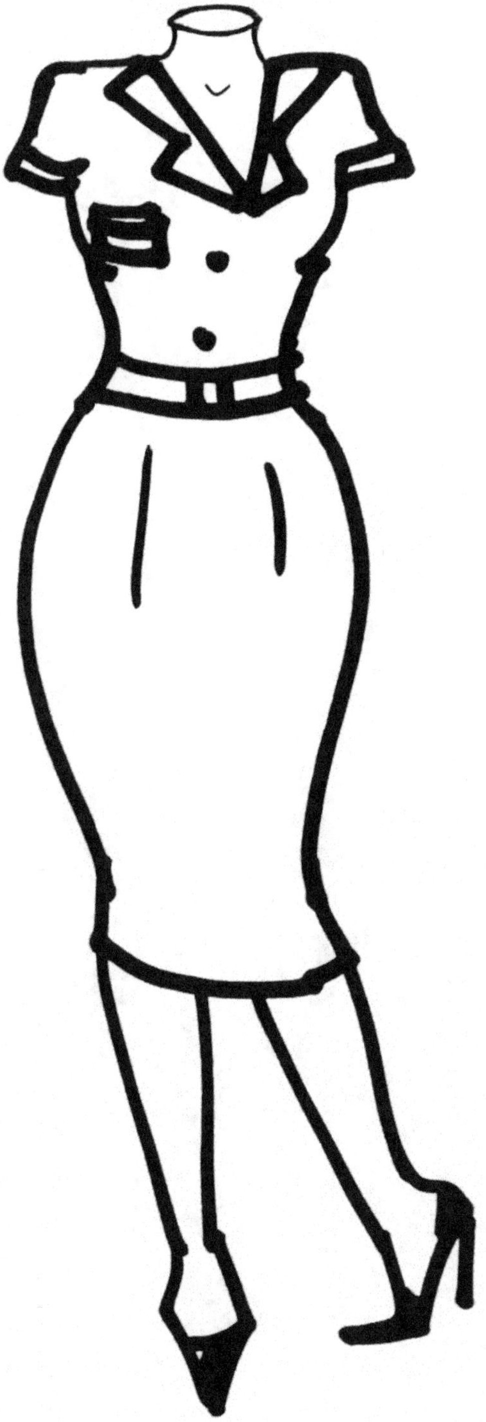

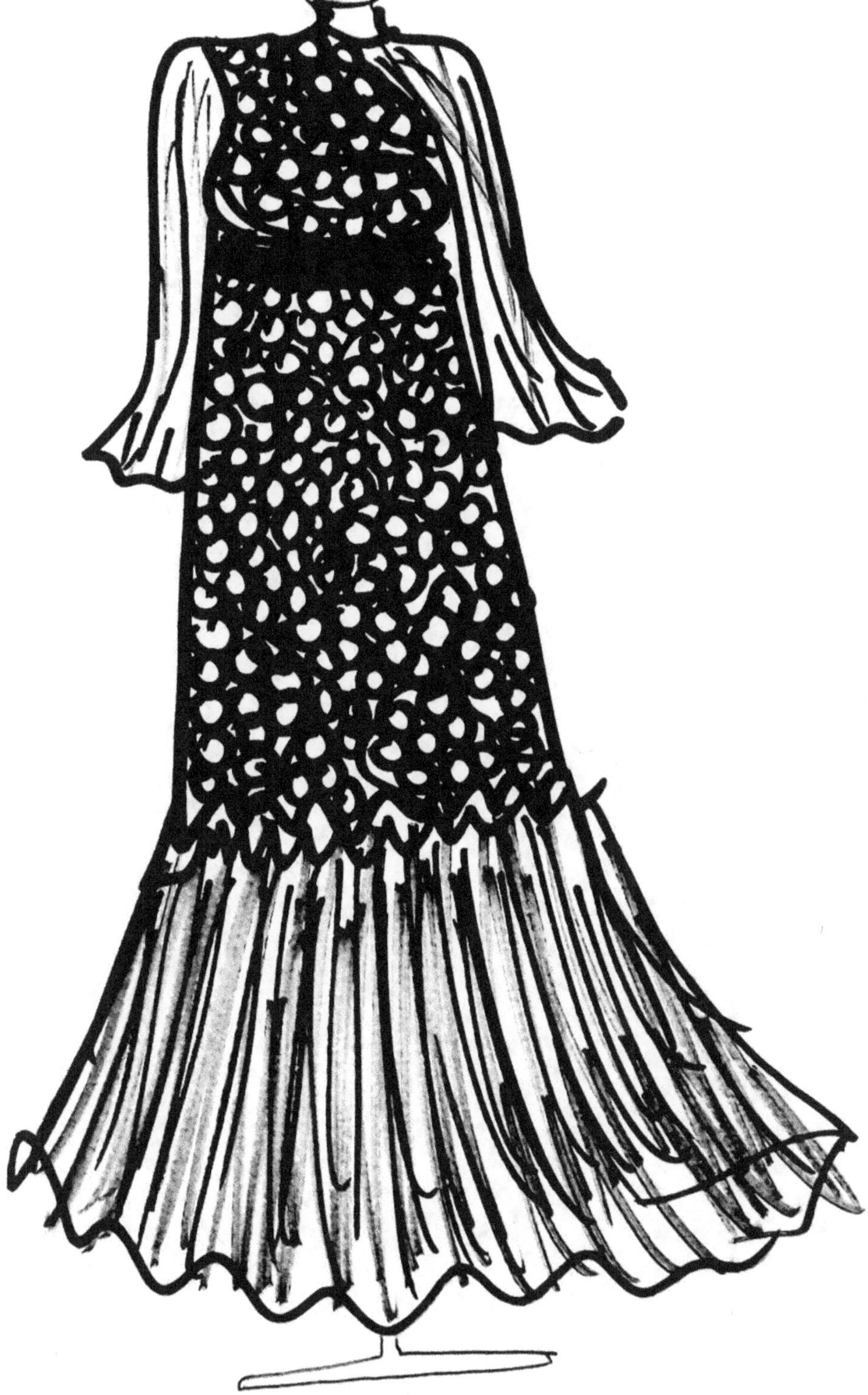

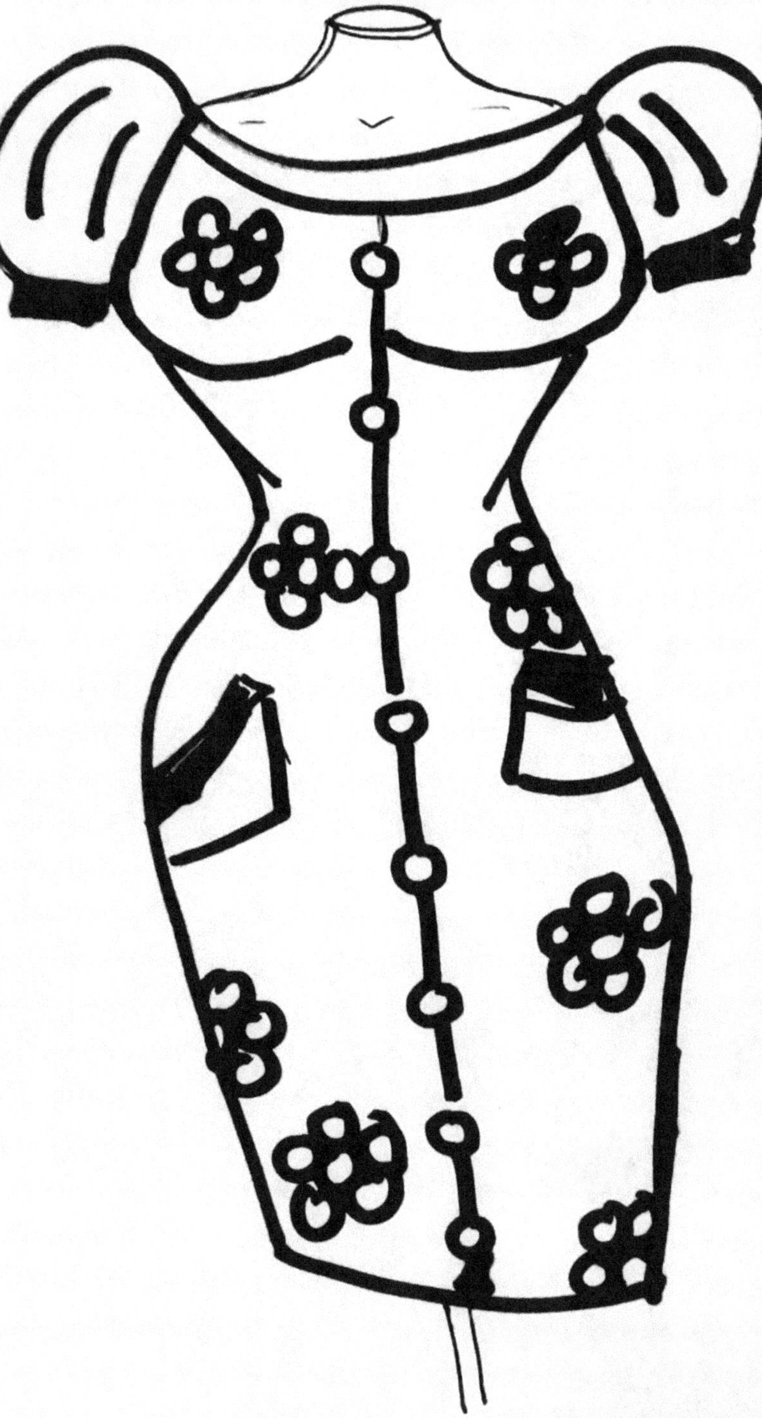

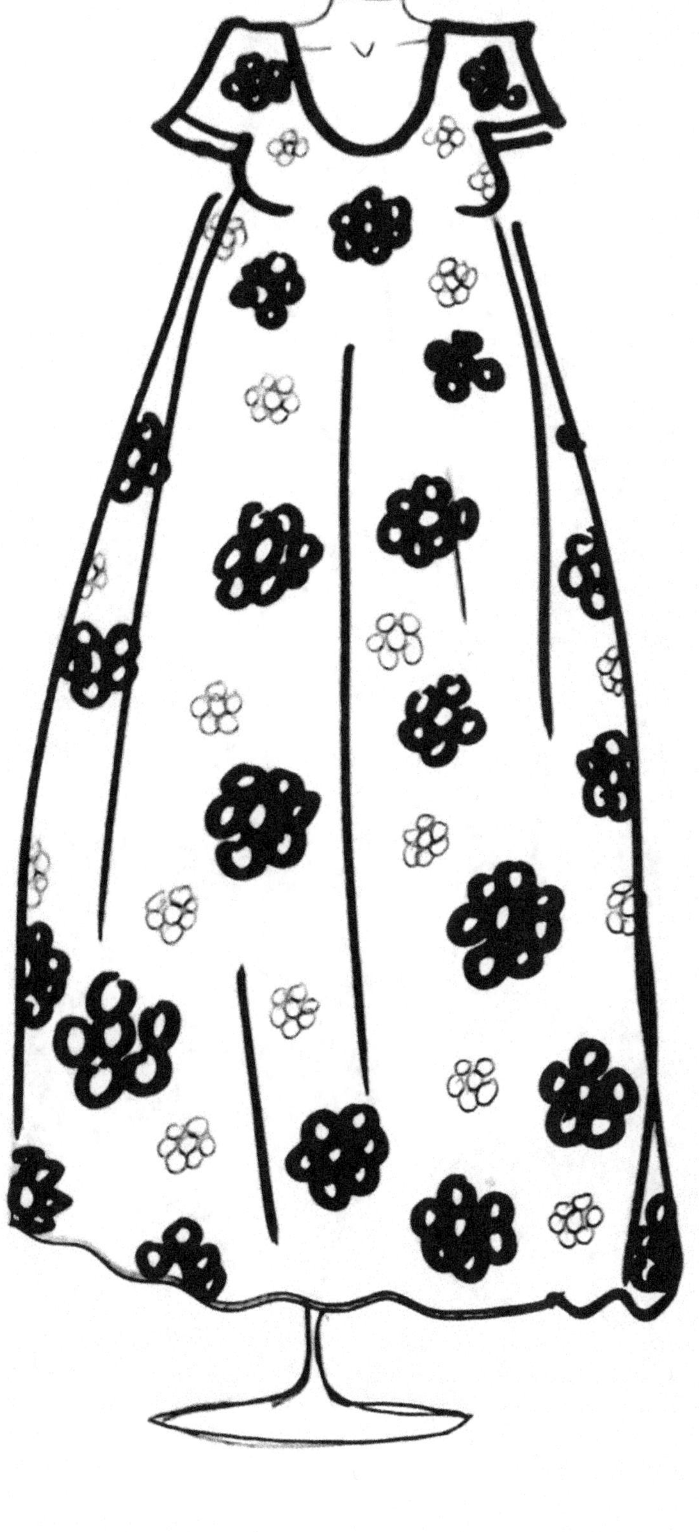

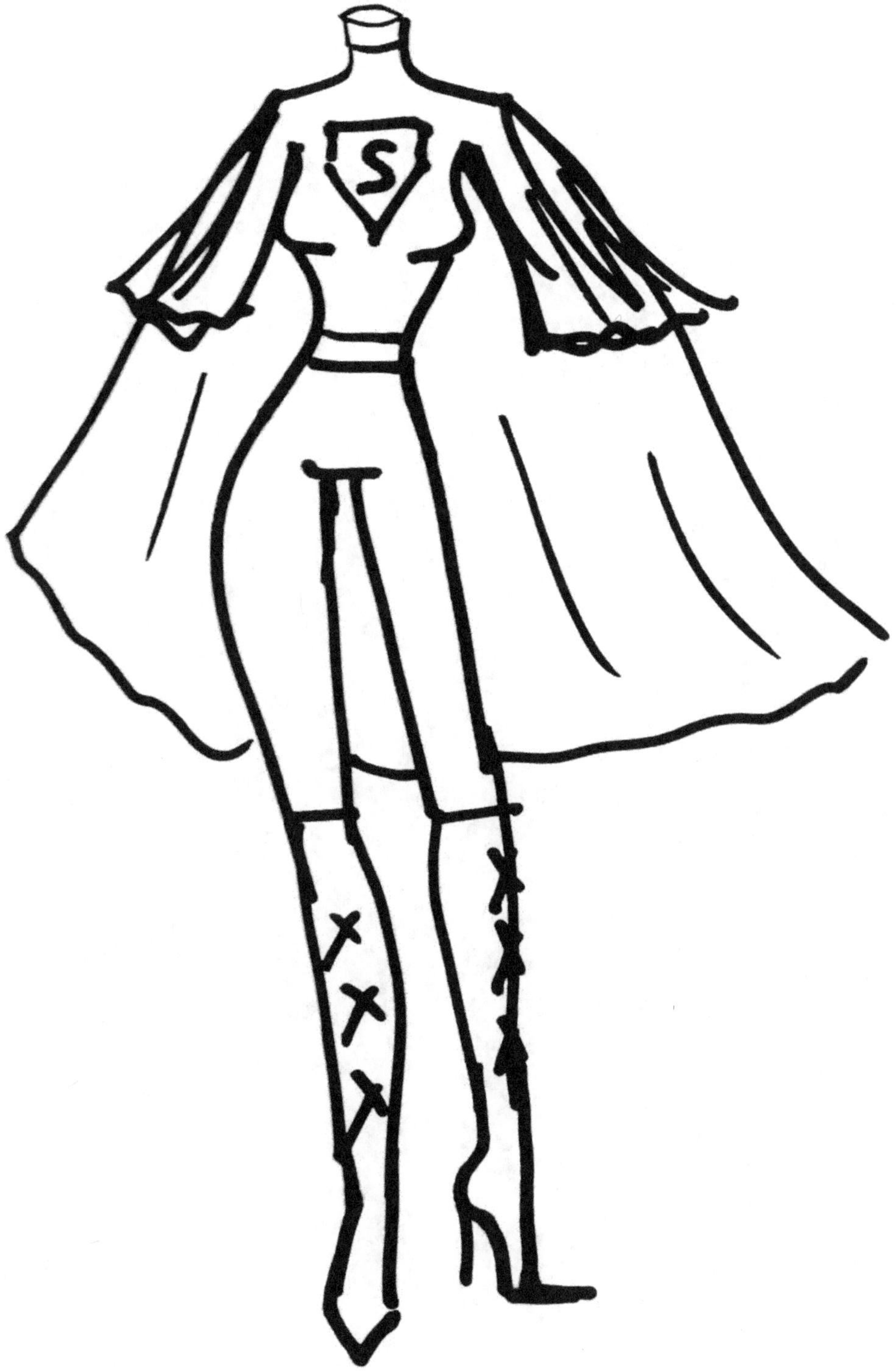
S

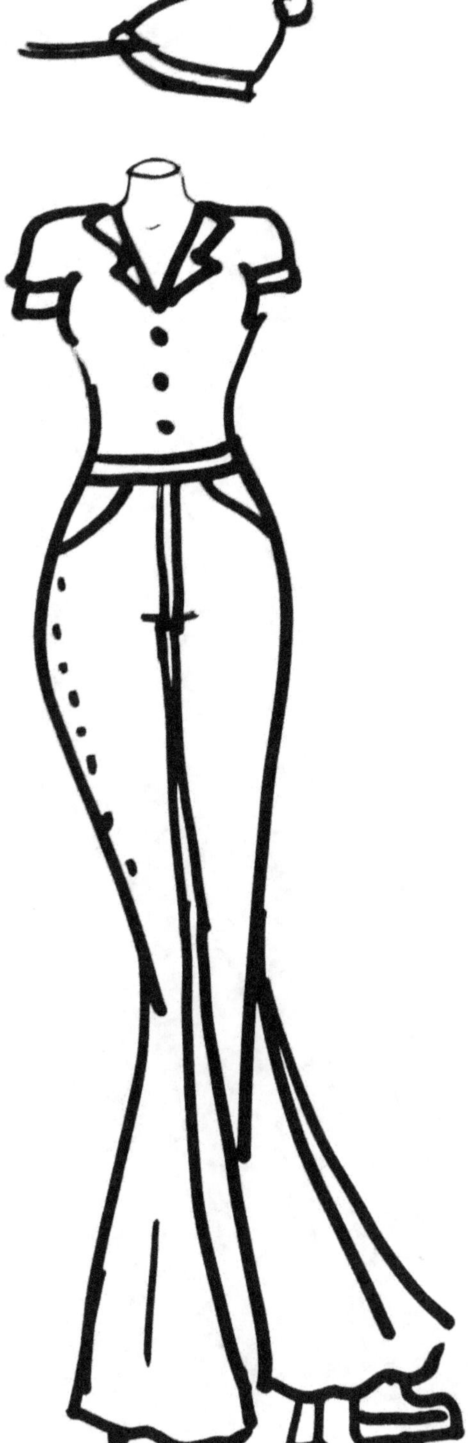

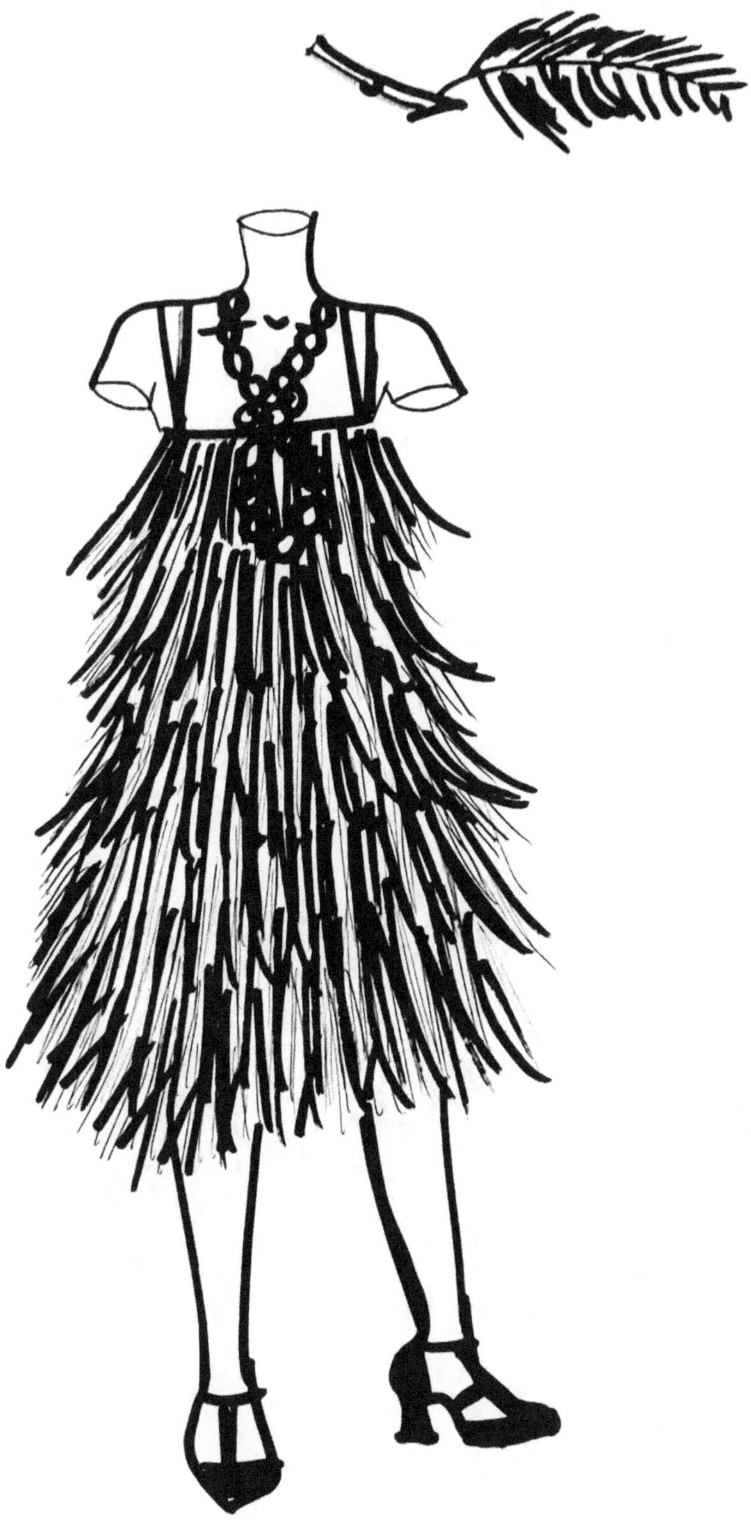

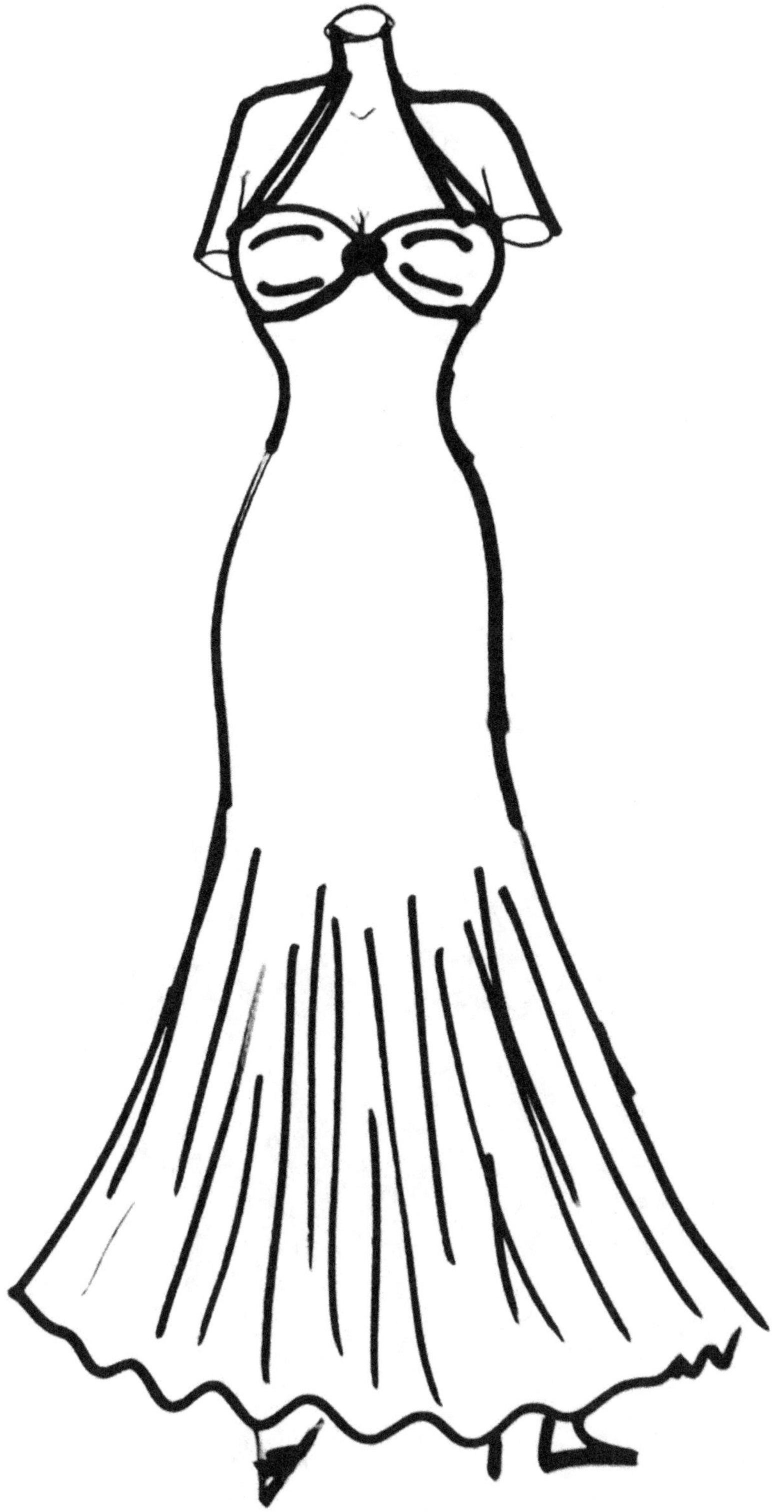

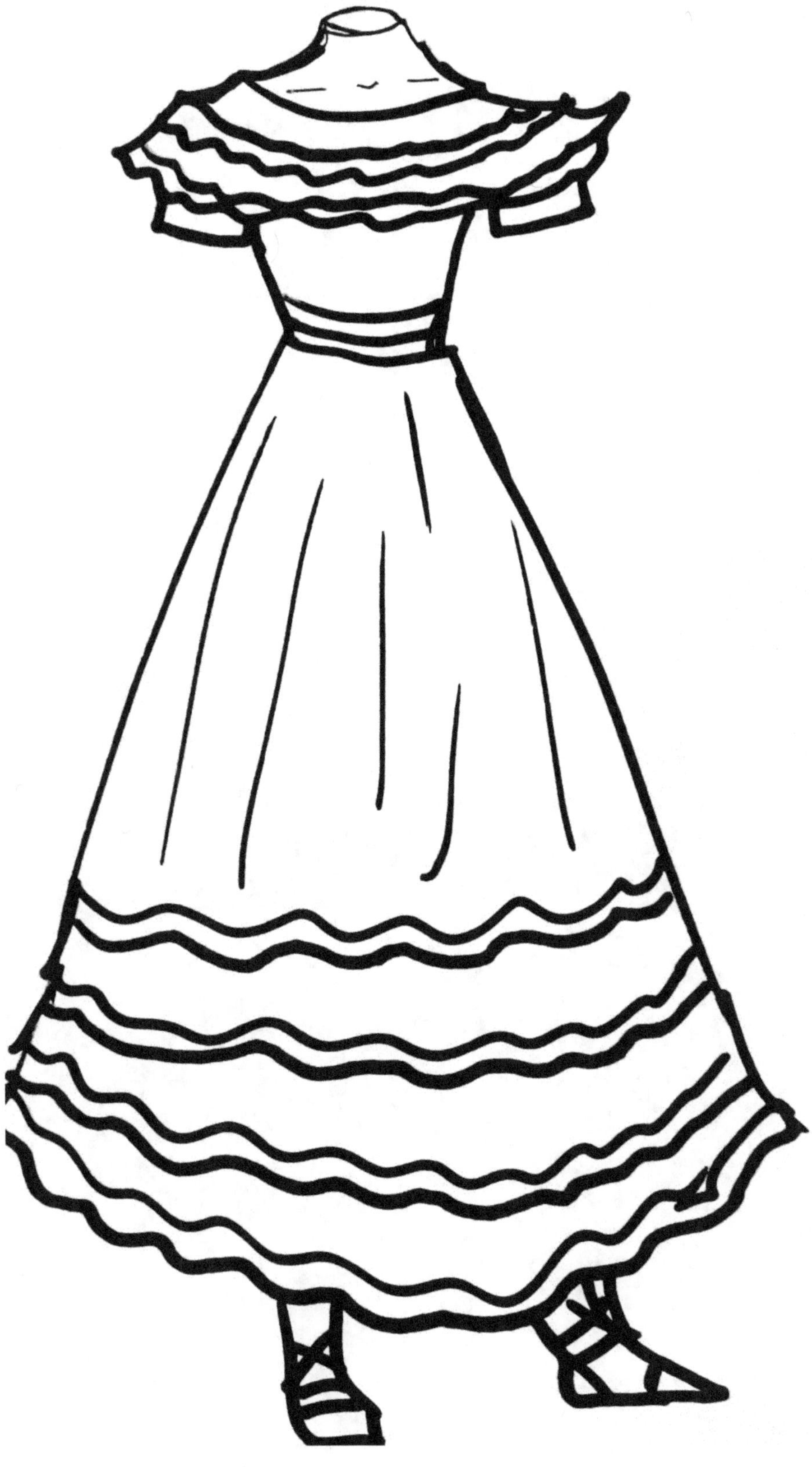

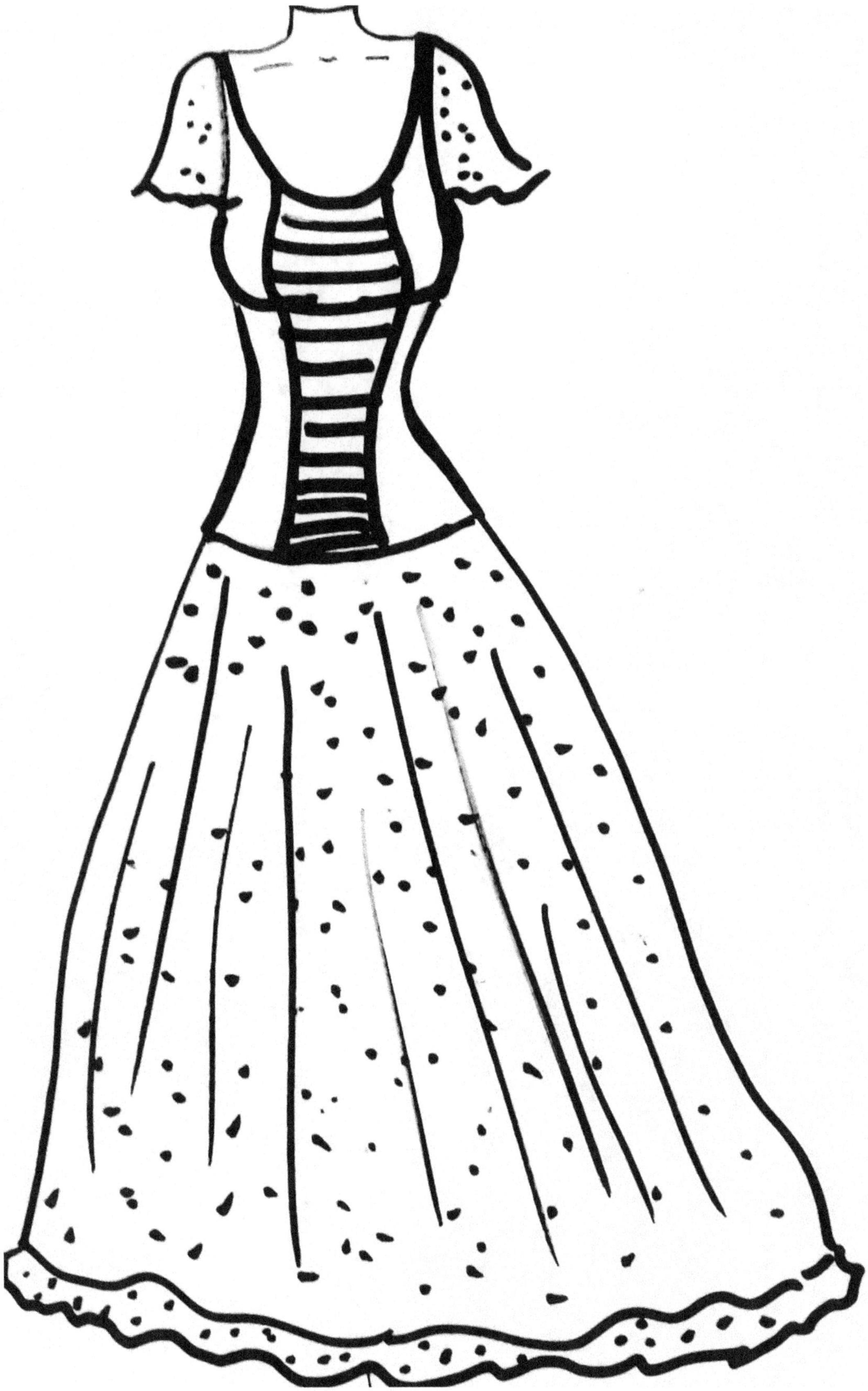

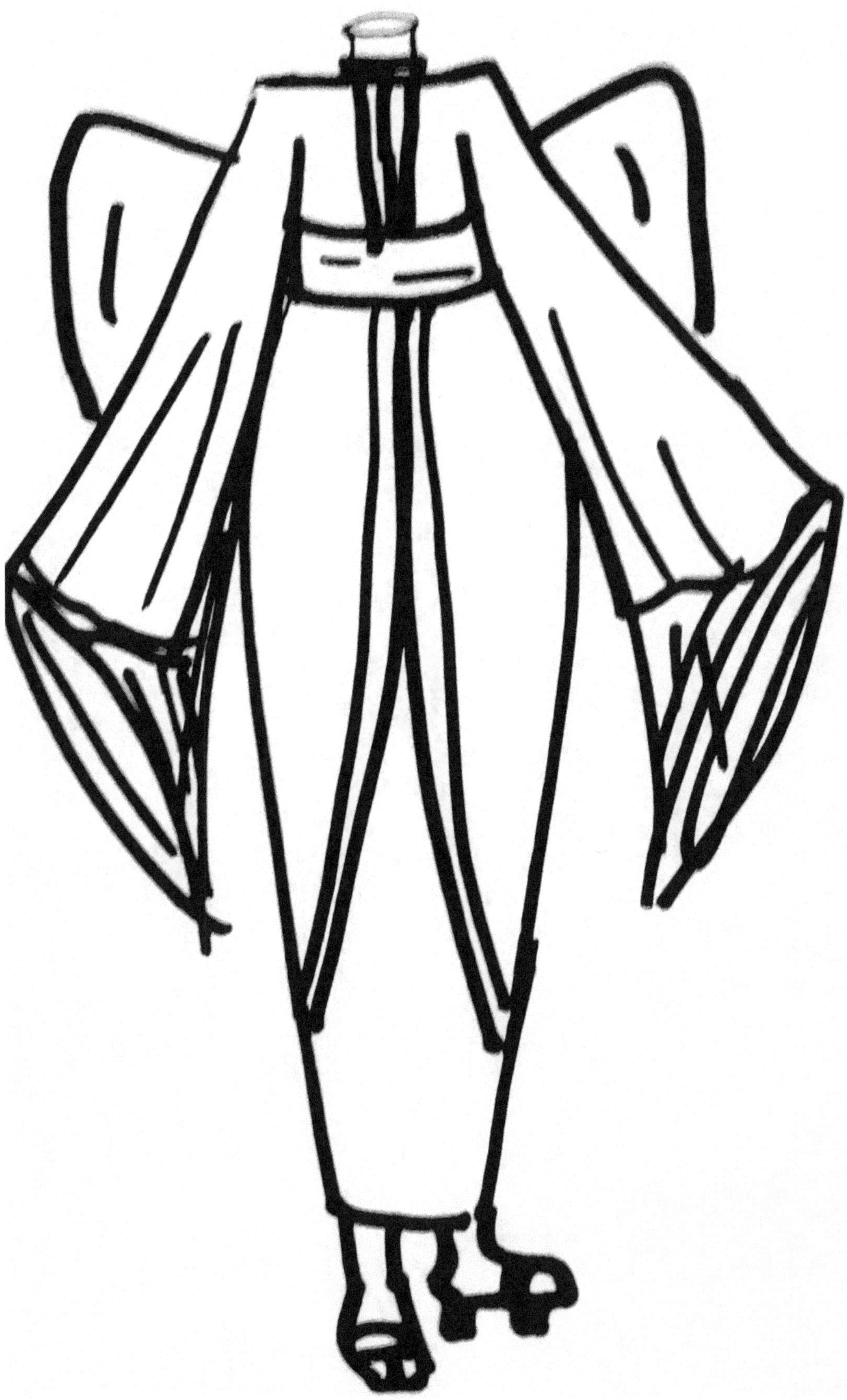

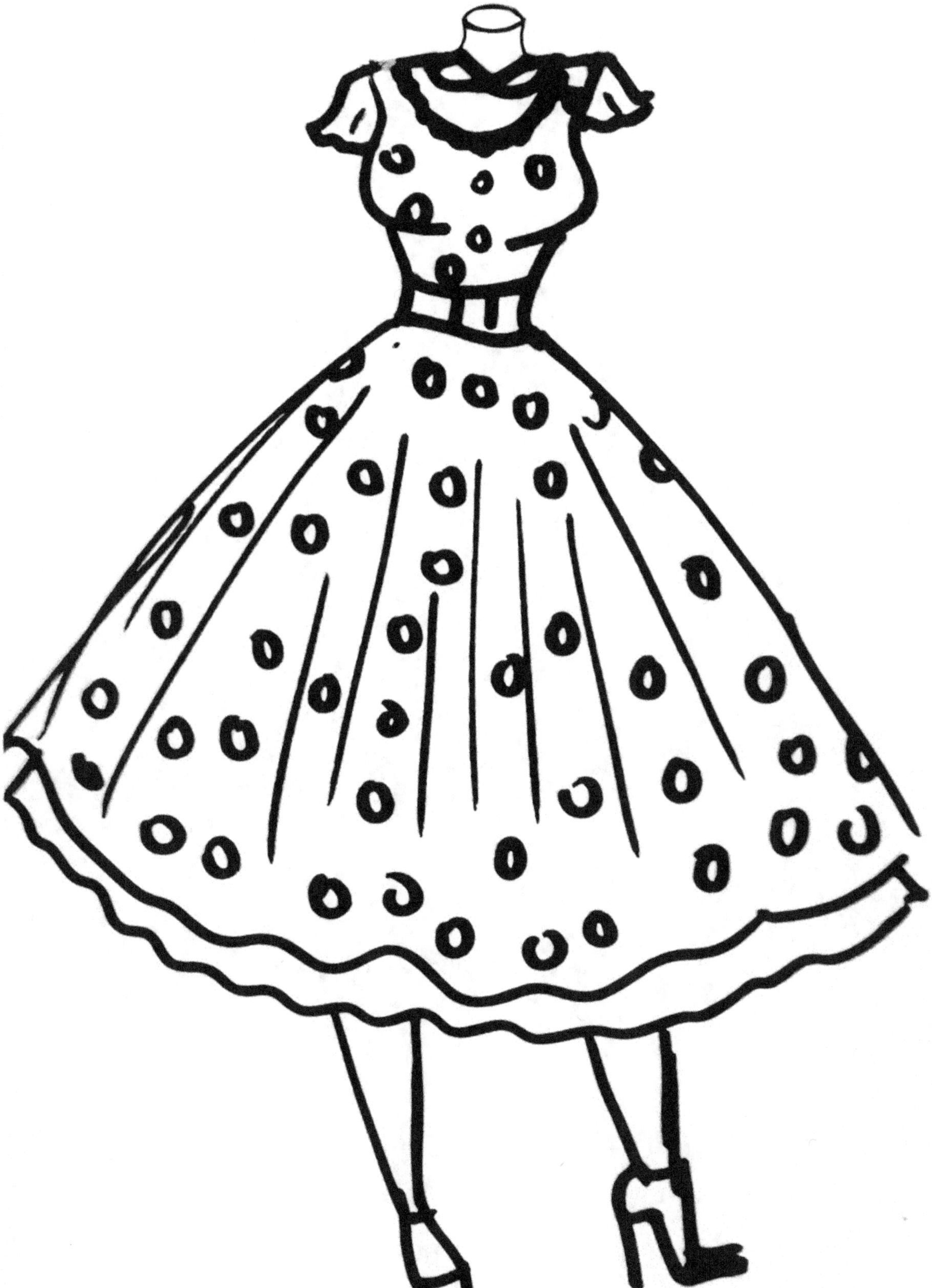

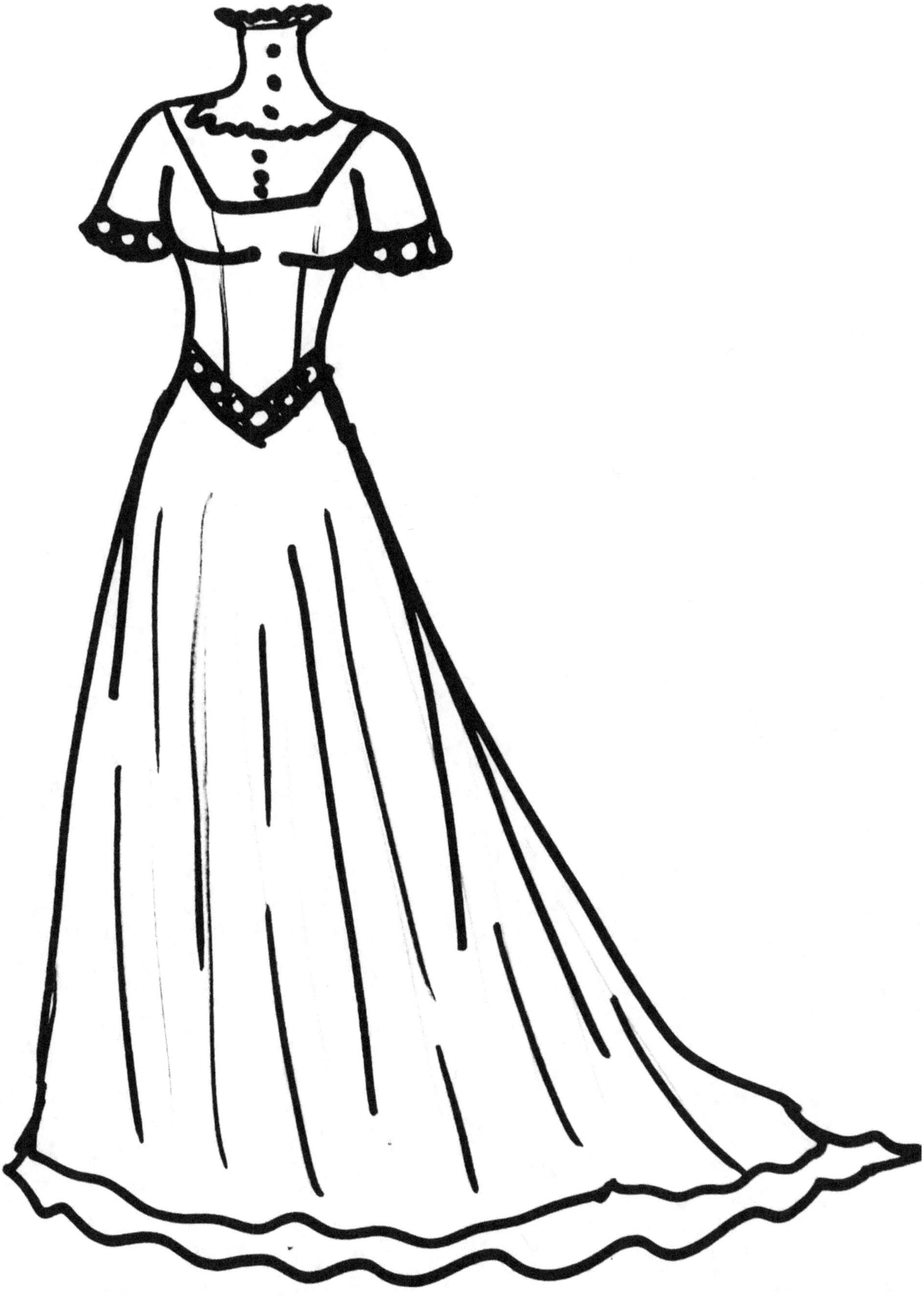

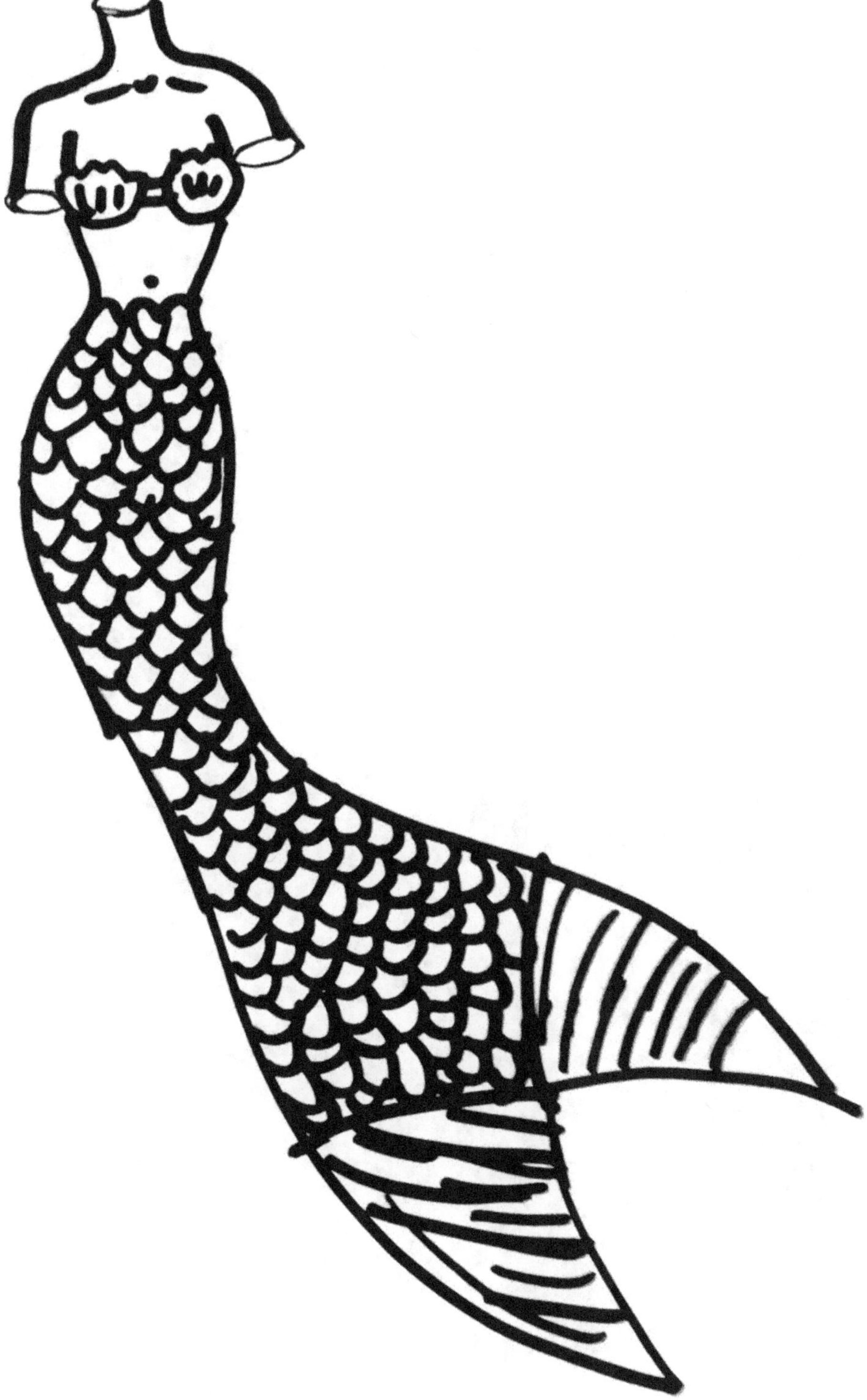

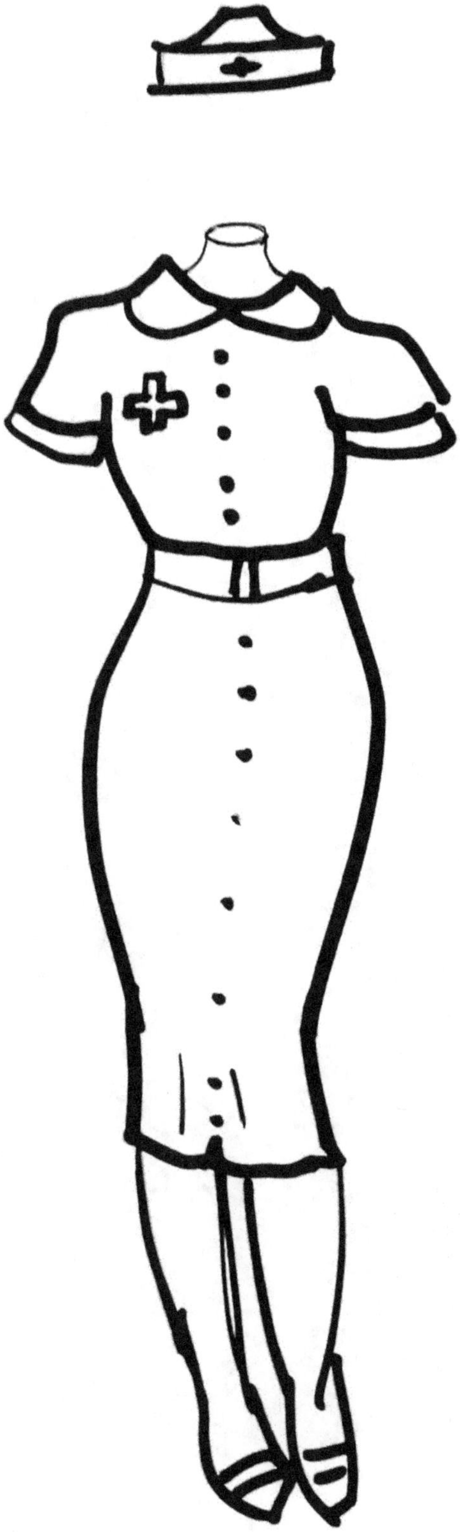

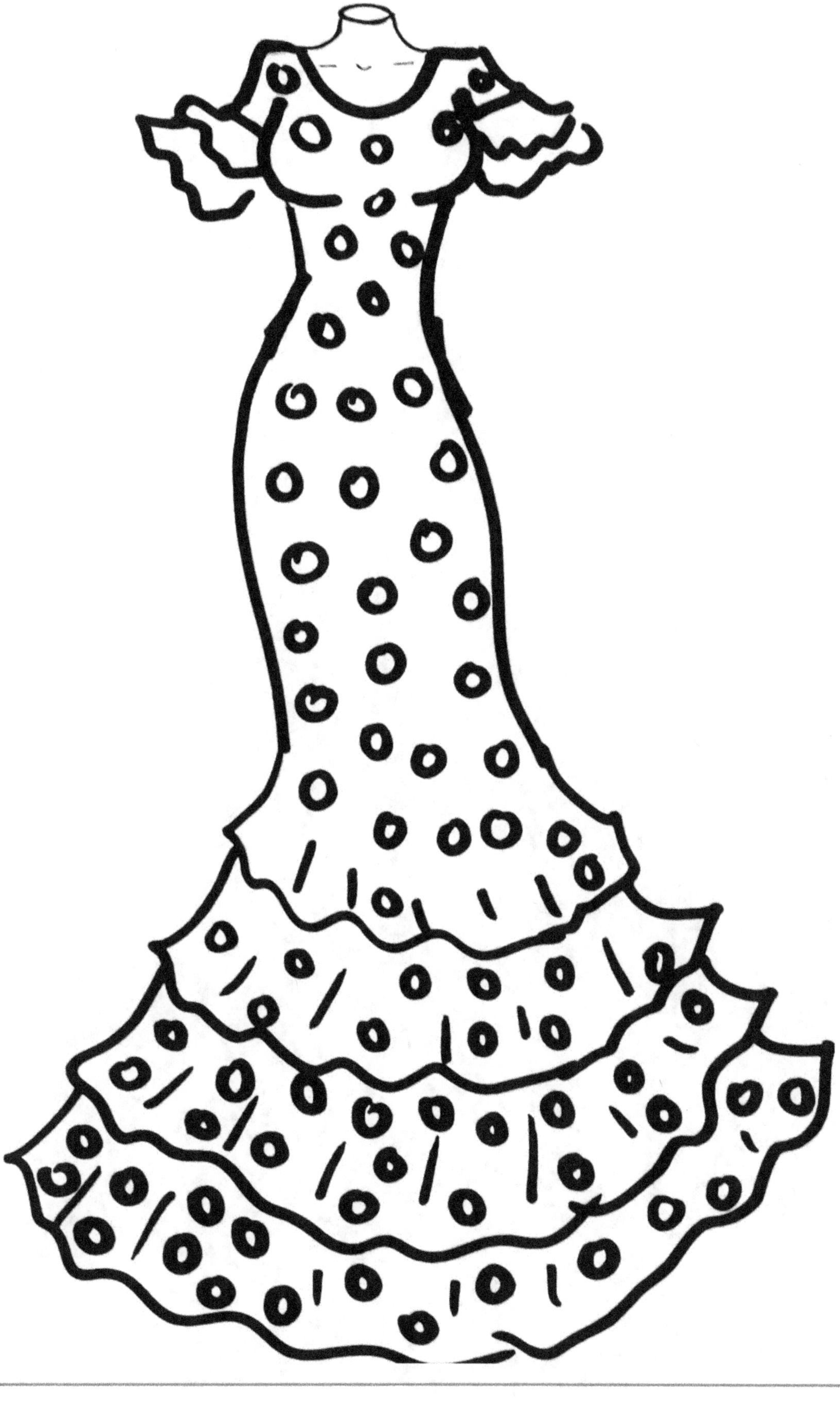

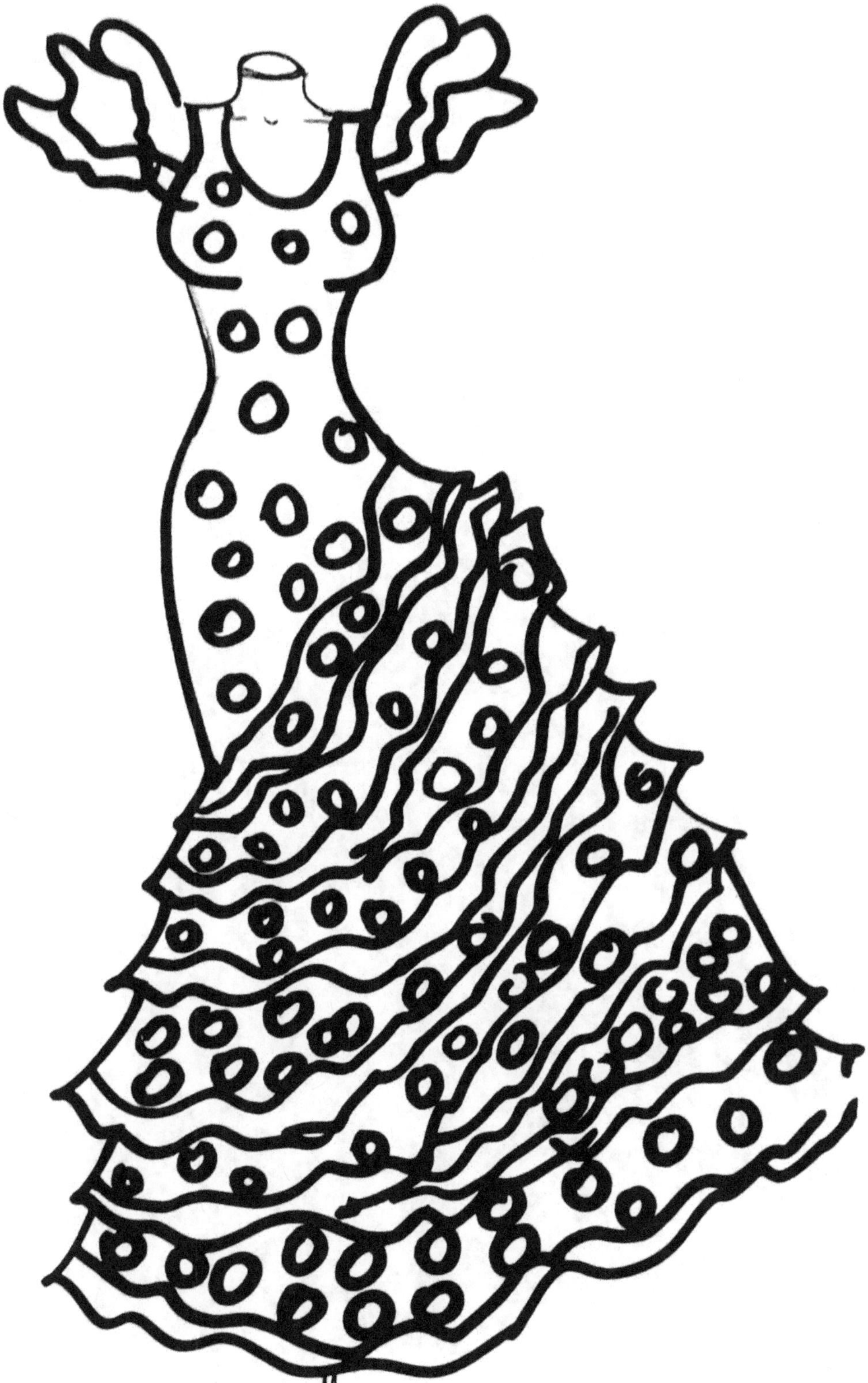

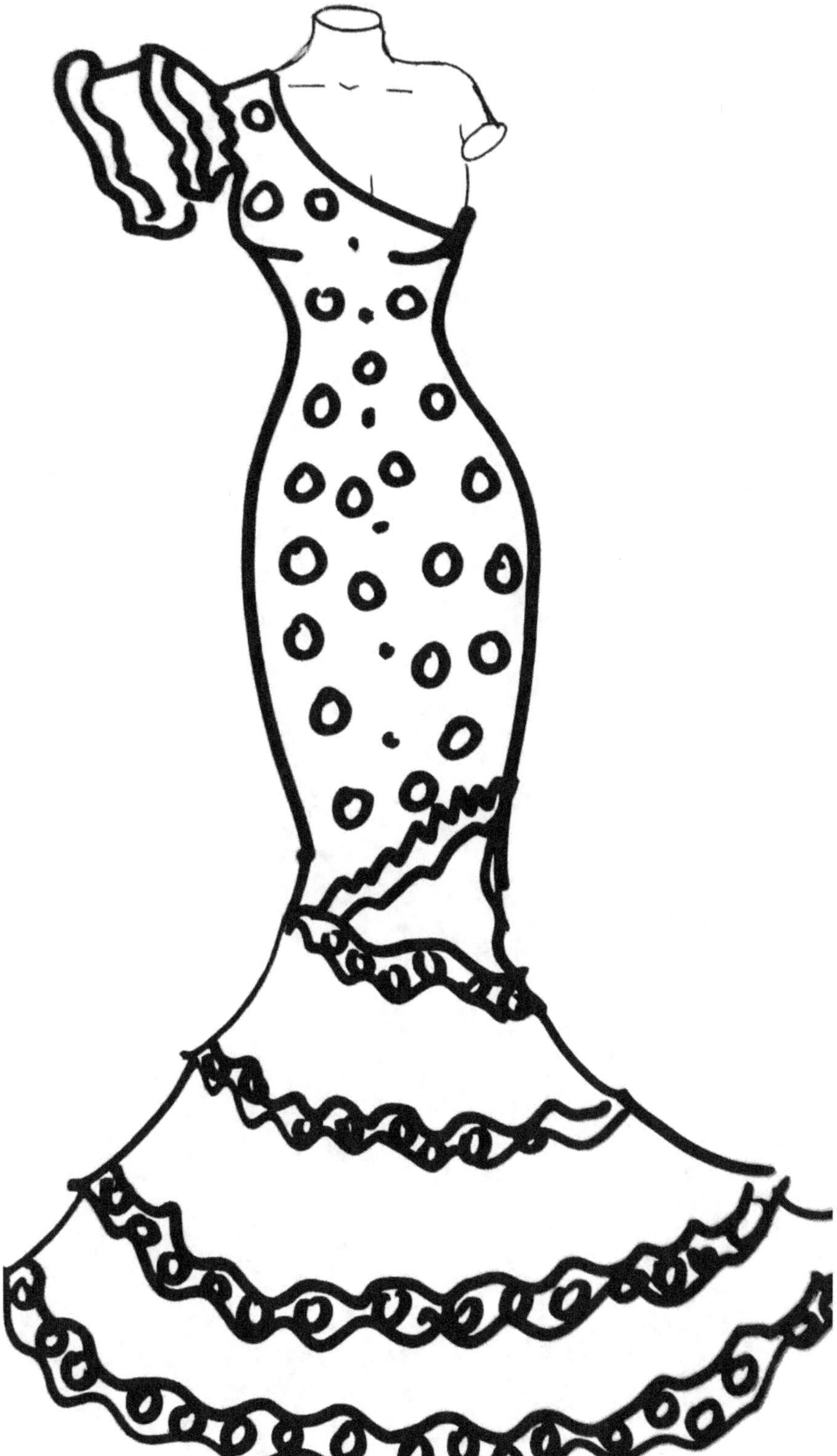

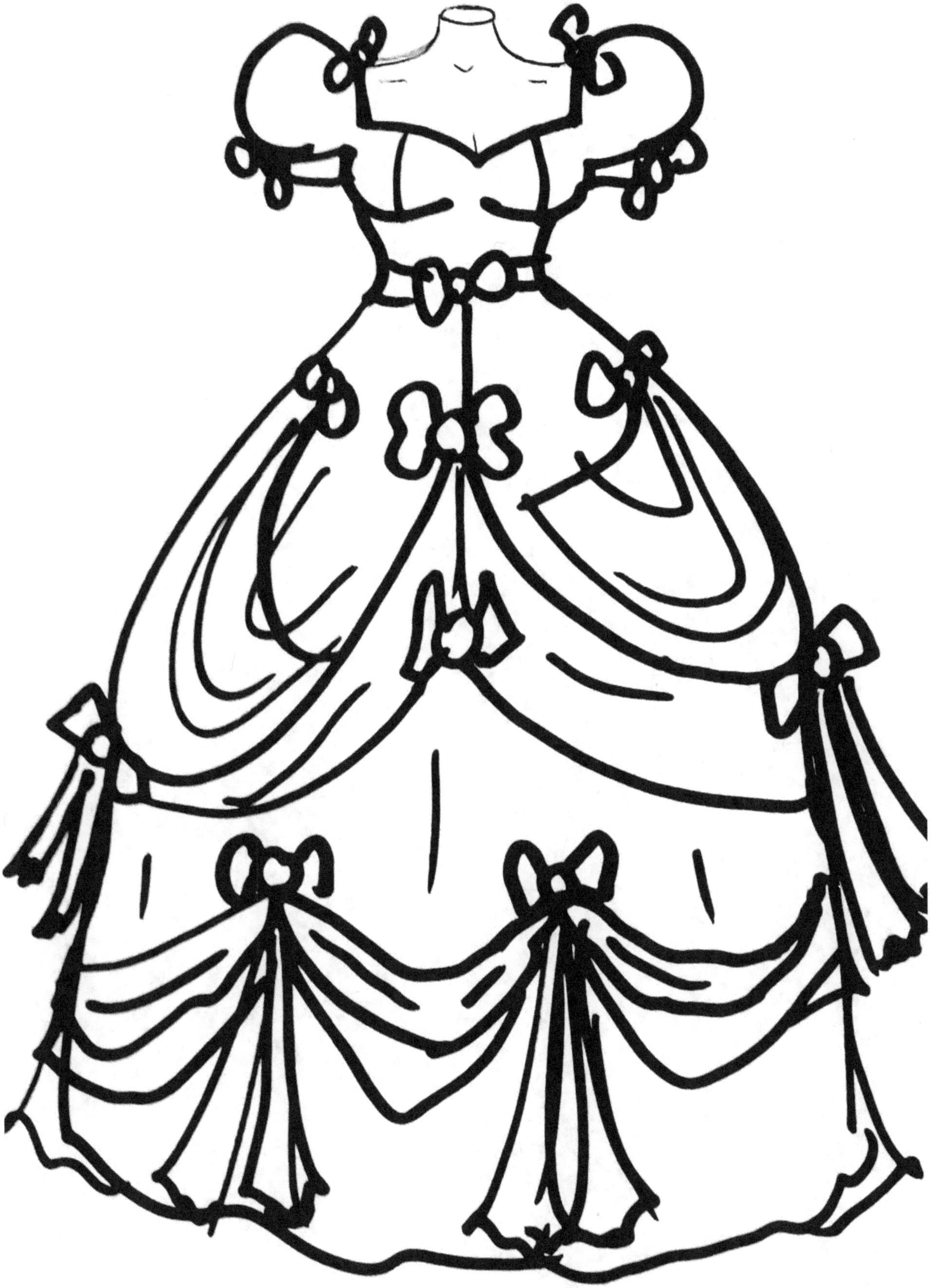

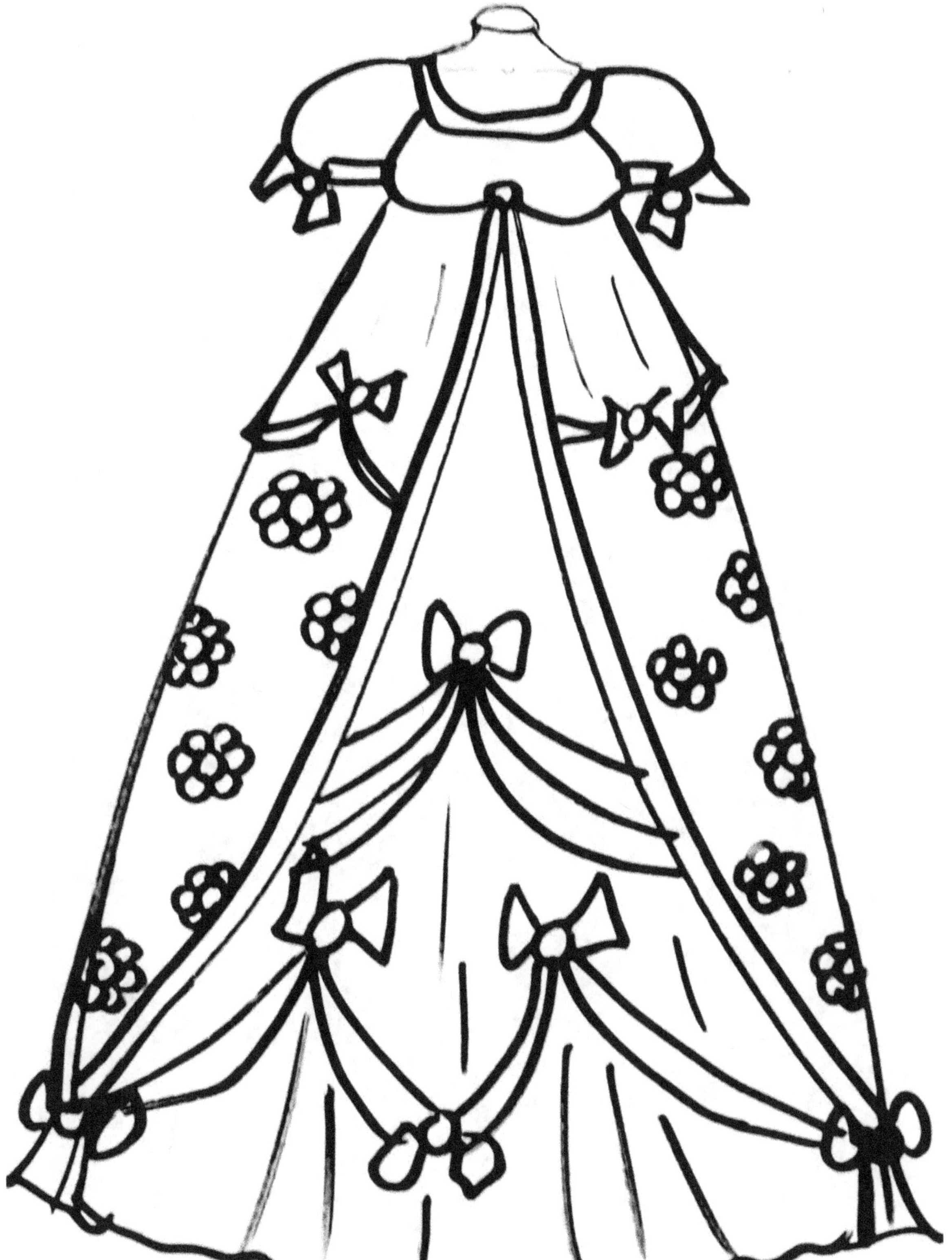

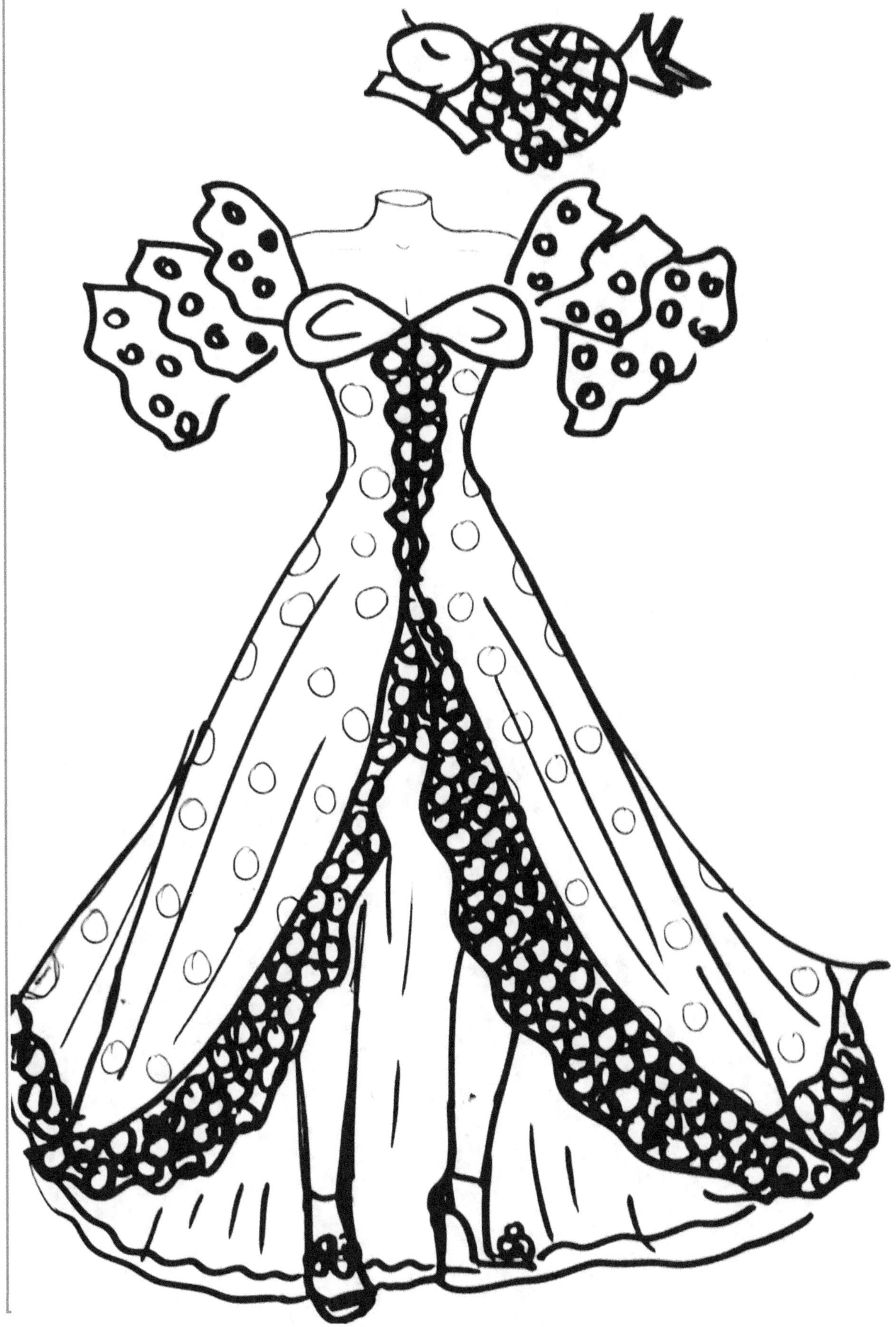

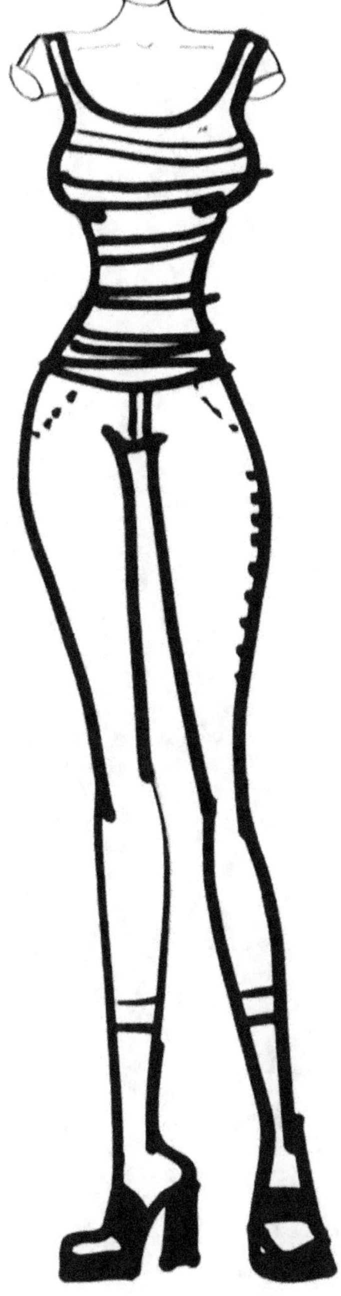

www.ingramcontent.com/pod-product-compliance
Lightning Source LLC
Chambersburg PA
CBHW081057240526
45465CB00025B/2506
* 9 7 9 8 3 7 4 7 0 2 5 6 9 *